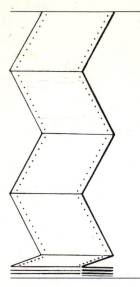

Ten-Statement
Spiral BASIC

From Calculator
to Computer

Glencoe Series in Computer Science and Data Processing

George Ledin Jr., Series Editor

Norman R. Lyons, *Structured COBOL for Data Processing*
Richard E. Mayer, *Ten-Statement Spiral BASIC: From Calculator to Computer*

Forthcoming:

Jack A. Fuller, *Business BASIC: Programming and Applications*
Curtis Gerald, *Introduction to Data Processing*
George Ledin Jr., *Fundamentals of Computer Science*
Mel Maron, *Numerical Methods for Calculators and Computers*
Joseph Paul, *Methods of Simulation for Dynamic Systems Engineering*
James Pick, *Business Data Processing*
Harvey L. Shapiro, *Introduction to Assembly Language Programming on the PDP 10 and the PDP 11*

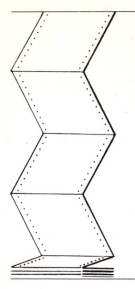

Ten-Statement Spiral BASIC

From Calculator to Computer

Richard E. Mayer
University of California, Santa Barbara

Glencoe Publishing Co., Inc.
Encino, California
Collier Macmillan Publishers
London

To Beverly, Kenneth, and David

Printed in the United States of America

Glencoe Publishing Co., Inc.
17337 Ventura Boulevard
Encino, California 91316
Collier Macmillan Canada, Ltd.

Library of Congress Catalog Card Number: 79-84624
1 2 3 4 5 6 7 8 9 10   83 82 81 80 79

ISBN 0-02-471560-3

Contents

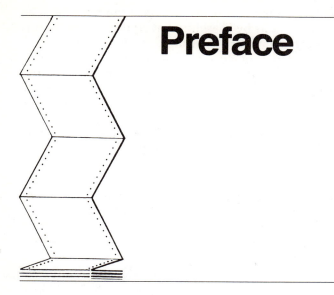

Preface

This book is written for anyone who wants to learn how to communicate with computers, and especially for the student with no background in computers or computer programming. People in business, science, and education—both in their work and their roles as consumers—are finding it more and more important to know something about computers, about what they can and cannot do. *Ten-Statement Spiral BASIC* will equip students with what is rapidly becoming a survival skill: a knowledge of how computers work.

This text can stand alone as an introduction to BASIC or can be used with other books; it can even serve as a primer for more advanced programming languages. *Ten-Statement Spiral BASIC* can also be used in introductory courses on statistics and quantitative methods given by departments of business, education, or social science.

Organization and Features. Because this text is aimed at the student new to computers, the introduction explains how a computer is like the familiar pocket calculator. Definitions of *hardware* and *software* are given, followed by an explanation of what computer languages are.

Chapter 1, "Inside the Computer," explains the five parts of a computer and what a program is. The next eight chapters introduce the student to ten statements used in BASIC, and also explain the use of character strings and the functions available in BASIC.

Now that classes in BASIC include future scientists, managers, and educators, as well as students training to be professional programmers, the method of instruction has become more important. To avoid overwhelming students by presenting everything at once, this text uses a *spiral approach*: a core of information is presented first, and more details are added only when this core is understood.

For example, the text begins by showing how to solve a unit-price problem on a pocket calculator. Each successive chapter overview shows how students can write progressively more sophisticated programs to solve this problem more efficiently, or to solve more complex versions of this problem. The spiral approach is particularly suited to BASIC, since BASIC lets students write and interpret programs from almost the first day of class, yet can also be used to teach more sophisticated programming techniques.

By beginning with the familiar pocket calculator and proceeding in small steps, this text keeps opportunities for frustration and misunderstanding at a minimum. Students working with computers for the first time will find that the nontechnical language and consistent format used throughout the text also make learning easier.

Because most of the delays and frustrations in using computers occur in trying to "debug" programs, this text teaches students how to "read" a program as well as how to "write" one. To interpret a program, a student must have a picture of what is happening inside the computer in response to each statement and chunk of statements in a program. The computer model presented in Chapter 1 enables students to find the errors in a program that won't run by visualizing what is happening inside the computer.

Learning Aids. Spiral learning is based on the student's mastering each concept before going on to the next. In *Ten-Statement Spiral BASIC* every major idea and every chapter is followed by an exercise designed to ensure mastery. Answers and explanations immediately follow each exercise, making it easy for students to pinpoint areas for review.

In addition to the chapter overviews already mentioned, students will find chapter summaries. These summaries demonstrate the student's progress by using the BASIC statements learned in each chapter to progressively construct and elaborate a computer gradebook.

Within the text itself, computer terms like *software* and *back-up memory* are printed in boldface, and repeated in the margin. Programming techniques (like *DATA statement* and *INTEGER function*) are highlighted by a computer console. These marginal devices let students quickly locate and review key terms and techniques. "Style Boxes" give students a concise presentation of essential formatting rules that must be memorized.

Several sections at the back of the book collect and summarize information presented throughout the text. An epilogue summarizes the student's progress on the unit-price problem, from the simple calculator computation to a complete and varied program in BASIC. A glossary collects the computer terms and programming techniques the student has learned.

Appendix A, "Operating Instructions," shows students how to get the programs they've written into and out of the computer. Appendix B, "Examples and Formats of the Ten BASIC Statements," shows what each BASIC statement should look like and what it can do. A "Comments" column lists important characteristics about how each statement is used. A manual planned to show instructors how to help students overcome "computer anxiety" is also available.

Acknowledgments. I would like to acknowledge the excellent support this project has received from the staff of Glencoe Publishing Company. George Gath has watched over and helped mold this book. Catherine Fuller supervised copy editing of the text and instructor's manual, and kept both on schedule during production. I greatly appreciate the help of George Ledin Jr., Glencoe's series editor in computer science and data processing, whose comments led to a manuscript much better than the original. I would also like to thank Ben Shneiderman (of the University of Maryland), John Gould and Lance Miller (of IBM), and my colleagues in the computer science departments at Indiana University and the University of California at Santa Barbara—all these people increased my interest in computer programming. Finally, I am grateful to my wife, Beverly, and to my sons, Kenneth and David, for giving me the time and encouragement needed to write this book.

Introduction: Hardware and Software

Calculators
The Computer
The Language

Calculators

It might be a good idea to start by exploring how much you already know about computers and computer programming. Although you may not have realized it, you probably have already had some "hands-on" experience with computers and programming. Have you ever used a pocket calculator? In the past decade they have become a part of everyday life. It is important for you to realize that pocket calculators are really just very simple computers. If you know how to use one, you are already well on your way to understanding how computers operate.

The incredible popularity of pocket calculators suggests that more powerful and probably much larger computers will become a part of our everyday lives in the near future. In order to build upon what you already know, let's first look at what we know about calculators. Although calculators seem to differ in the features they offer, a typical pocket calculator has ten digit keys (for entering numbers), four function keys (for adding, subtracting, multiplying, and dividing), a clear key, an equals key, a memory 1 entry key, a memory 1 recall key, a memory 2 entry key, a memory 2 recall key, and an eight-space readout display. Figure 1 gives a representation of our simple pocket calculator. Does it look familiar?

1

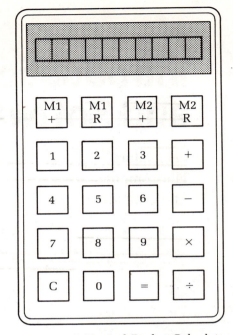

Figure 1.   A Typical Pocket Calculator.

hardware
software

In this chapter you will learn about the parts of a computer (the hardware) and about how to communicate with a computer using a programming language (the **software**).

To understand computer hardware, try to think of the components in your pocket calculator.

First, there must be some way to get information into the machine; this function is accomplished by some input device. In our calculator, the input device is the keyboard, and in a computer system the input device can be a computer terminal or a card reader.

Second, there must be some way to get information out of the calculator; this function is accomplished by some output device. In our calculator the output device is the digital readout display, and in a computer system the output device can be a terminal or a paper printer.

Also, there must be some way to hold information in memory; this is performed by some memory device. In our calculator, the memory is inside the calculator but there is not much of it; in a computer system, the memory can be a large space inside the computer or a magnetic disk or tape outside of the computer.

Finally, there must be some way to perform arithmetic operations and to control the order in which they are executed; this is accomplished by the central processing unit (CPU). In our pocket calculator, the only operations are add, subtract, multiply, and divide,

Courtesy of Texas Instruments

and the order in which they are performed is controlled by our fingers; in large computer systems the CPU can perform many more kinds of operations, and the order in which they are performed is controlled by a program.

To understand computer software, try to think of how you instruct a pocket calculator. Let's say you want to find the unit price (i.e., price per ounce) of a 12-ounce jar of peanut butter that costs $1.03. Your sequence of operations would be the following:

>   enter 103 in the digit keys
>   press divide key
>   enter 12 in the digit keys
>   press equals key

On the readout you would see 103 (cents), then 12 (ounces), then 8.5833333 (cents per ounce).

If you want to use your calculator's memory so that you can recall the cost and ounces, you would follow this sequence of operations:

>   enter 103 in the digit keys
>   press memory 1 entry key
>   enter 12 in the digit keys
>   press memory 2 entry key
>   press memory 1 recall key
>   press divide key
>   press memory 2 recall key
>   press equals key

In this case you first put the price and ounces in memory, and then you recall them for use in your computation. The final readout would be 8.5833333.

Actually, the preceding list of operations is a computer program. A computer program is simply a list of things to do. The computer starts at the top and goes down the list in order. In BASIC computer programming, you simply list the steps in order using a very limited set of words. When the computer executes your program, it follows the program step by step, doing each operation that is specified. Thus when you write a program in BASIC you are just telling the computer to perform a list of operations such as entering a number into a memory space, recalling a number from a memory space, performing an arithmetic operation, showing the results, and so forth.

The Computer

Definition. A computer is simply a device for the electronic storage, manipulation, and production of symbols, upon command. For example, as was pointed out in the previous section, a simple pocket calculator fits this definition—it stores, manipulates, and produces numerical symbols, it is electronic, and it operates on your command.

History. Although the history of mechanical "computing machines" begins in the past century, the first electronic computers did not go into operation until the 1940s. In 1946 a computer called ENIAC was introduced, and it was quite an impressive sight. ENIAC—for Electronic Numerical Integrator And Computer—consisted of almost 20,000 vacuum tubes, it weighed 30 tons, it required massive amounts of electricity, and it took up as much space as a small house. ENIAC also had a characteristic that distinguished it from anything that had been built before—it could make 5,000 calculations in a single second. A commercial version of this computer—called UNIVAC-1—became available in 1951.

A major technological problem with these computers was that the vacuum tubes kept burning out, were bulky, generated too much heat, and consumed great amounts of electricity. In other words, vacuum tubes would not make it today in our energy-conscious world. A major breakthrough came in the development of transistors to replace vacuum tubes. Transistors were much smaller, cheaper, cooler, and more reliable. Soon computers were built using transistors instead of vacuum tubes.

In 1965, a computer was built that included improvements even better than transistors—integrated circuits. This computer, the PDP-8, manufactured by the Digital Equipment Corporation, revolutionized computing machinery in the same way that the Volkswagen Beetle revolutionized automotive motoring. (In case you are curious, PDP stands for "Programmable Data Processor.") It was now possible to produce complex integrated circuits on small silicon chips such that one square inch contained the equivalent of hundreds of transistors. Computers built with integrated circuits (ICs) were much smaller and cheaper than any of the earlier computers, and yet they could perform 500,000 computations per second.

A third major improvement over the vacuum tube occurred in the early 1970s when Intel Corporation produced a microprocessor chip—thousands of circuits were compacted into a chip smaller than one square inch. By 1975, the first low-cost, microprocessor computer—the Altair 8800—was commercially available. Since then dozens of other models have been marketed. Today for less than a thousand dollars you can buy a computer that will sit on the top of your desk and yet has the computational power of the UNIVAC-1.

Components. While a blood and guts description is not needed, you should take a minute to learn about the main parts of the computer and what general function is performed by each. Computers

come in all sizes, shapes, colors, and levels of ability, but they generally have the following components:

Input. There must be some device similar to the keyboard on a pocket calculator for getting information into the computer's memory. Typical input devices for computer systems are **terminal keyboards,** card readers for punched (perforated) data cards, or readers for magnetic tape, paper tape, and magnetic disks.

terminal keyboards

Output. There must be some device similar to the digital read-out display on a pocket calculator for communication from the computer to the outside world. Typical output devices include the **terminal screen,** a printer that gives you "hard copy" (that is, typed paper), or a card punch. Quite often the same device (for example, a terminal) can be used for both input and output. In general, input and output devices are separate from the central computer, and thus they are called peripheral devices.

terminal screen

Memory. A third component of any computer system must be something for storing information for future use or repeated use. Some memory will be located in the central computer—this is called the **main** or **core memory.** But an unlimited amount of additional memory can be attached to the central computer through peripheral devices—this is called **secondary** or **back-up memory.** Typical peripheral devices for back-up memory are magnetic disks, magnetic tape, paper tape, and punched cards.

main or core memory

back-up memory

Central Processing Unit. There must be some device for carrying out the "thinking" of a computer (such as performing arithmetic or logical operations) and also for determining the order in which the operations are to be performed. These "thinking" activities occur within the **central processing unit** (CPU). One part of the CPU determines the order in which statements in the program will be executed—this is the **executive control component.** Another part carries out the arithmetic and logical operations such as adding two numbers or deciding whether one number is larger than another—this is the *arithmetic and logic component.*

central processing unit
executive control component

In general, the main computer contains the CPU (executive control and arithmetic and logic components) and some core memory. Peripheral devices connected to the main computer contain back-up memory and input and output devices. This configuration is shown in Figure 2. It is possible to include all of these parts in one unit—our pocket calculator is an example.

Let's consider some typical hardware configurations involving these four components. Figure 3 shows a typical configuration; the

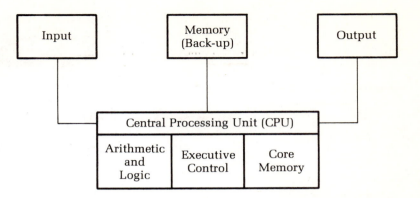

Figure 2. *The Four Components of a Computer System.*

input device is a terminal keyboard, the output device is a line printer, the back-up memory is stored on magnetic tape, and the CPU includes core memory, arithmetic/logic, and executive control. Figure 4 shows another configuration; the input device is a punched card reader, the output device is a printer, and the back-up memory consists of magnetic disks. While the particular configuration you work with may influence how large a program you can write, it really does not influence how you use the BASIC language. You would still get your instructions (program) into the computer through an input device, get the computer's response from an output device, and the operations would take place in the CPU.

Modes of operation.   In order to better understand how the components of a computer fit together, let's look at some typical situations

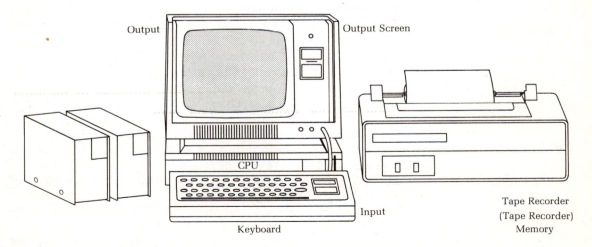

Figure 3.   *A Typical Stand-Alone Computer System. The CPU is built into the console.*

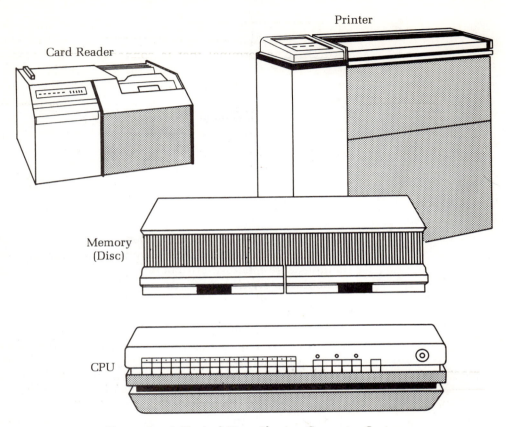

Figure 4.   *A Typical Time-Sharing Computer System.*

that you might be in when you communicate with a computer. When you use a pocket calculator you have the input, output, memory, and CPU right there in your hand and each operation you ask for is done immediately. However, when you use a terminal at a computer center, there may be many other people using the same system. This **time sharing** is called **time sharing** because the computer shares its time among many users, giving each user a time "slice." Suppose you are sitting in front of a computer terminal with a keyboard and screen, and you want to use the computer at your local computer center. The computer may be in another building (or even in another city), but you can communicate with it by telephone or through direct wires.

stand-alone   An alternative to time sharing is the use of a **stand-alone** computer. This means that you are the only one using the computer—you have your own personal computer. For most practical purposes it does not matter whether you are using a time-sharing system or a stand-alone system—the BASIC language is used in the same way and you get the same results.

Whether you are using a time-sharing or stand-alone system, there are several *modes* you can program in. Let's say you are sitting in front of a terminal that is connected with a computer system (either time-sharing or stand-alone). You could first enter your entire program and all the needed data and then ask the computer to execute it. This is called the **batch mode**—in this case you give the computer all it needs at once, and you have no further interaction with the computer. This is the mode you would normally use when doing the programming described in most of this book. Another way to use the computer is in the **interactive mode**—in this case you can interact with the computer as it runs a program. It may ask you questions, you may give answers, and vice versa. This is the communication mode used by a ticket reservationist when trying to book your airline reservations. This mode is covered in Chapter 7 of this book. A third mode is the **immediate mode**—in this case you may enter a command and the computer will execute it immediately. This is the mode in which your pocket calculator operates and is covered in Chapter 9 of this book.

batch mode

interactive mode

immediate mode

The Language

Computers are not born knowing any sophisticated language. A new computer can be given instructions, but the instructions must be in **machine language.** Machine language generally looks like strings of number and letter combinations in which each string makes possible some simple operation inside the computer. It is possible to program a computer using machine language, but you would need to know a lot about how the computer is built, and such programs are very hard to read.

machine language

Fortunately, many **programming languages** have been developed in which a statement is translated by a special program into a series of machine language symbols for the computer. Thus when you use a programming language, there is a program that translates the statements you wrote into machine language. In this way, programming languages (such as BASIC) allow you to instruct the computer in a language that is similar to English. This makes it easier for you to write and to interpret programs. Figure 5 shows the translation process from programming language to machine language.

programming languages

There are many programming languages: FORTRAN, APL, PL/1, COBOL, SNOBOL, PASCAL, ALGOL, and LISP are examples. Some are special-purpose languages that are most helpful in particular situations, while others have a more general purpose. Why should you begin with BASIC? First, BASIC is designed as a general-purpose language for beginners and is easy to learn. (BASIC was developed and copyrighted by John Kemeny and Thomas Kurtz of Dartmouth University in 1965.) In fact, BASIC stands for "Beginner's

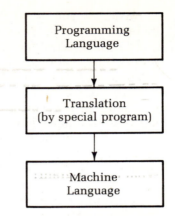

Figure 5.   Programming Language and Machine Language.

All-purpose Symbolic Instruction Code." Second, BASIC is one of the most widely available and popular languages. Most of the small microprocessor computers now on the market are programmable only in BASIC. (Each computer, of course, is always also programmable in its own machine language.) Thus you will be learning a language that can be used on just about every computer. Third, you can easily build on what you have learned in BASIC. The essentials of BASIC are really quite straightforward, and you can increase your programming skills easily. Thus BASIC is a language that you can grow with, writing simple programs at first and then much more powerful and sophisticated ones. Fourth, BASIC is a good primer for learning other, more difficult and specialized languages, and just for learning how computers work.

A word of caution, however, is in order at this point. Not all versions of BASIC are alike. Each computer manufacturer provides a slightly different version of BASIC. In most cases the differences are quite minor, but you occasionally have to consult the particular manual for your computer's version of BASIC. This book will allow you to refer to such manuals with confidence. The BASIC you will learn from this book is consistent with all major versions of BASIC and with the standards for "Minimal BASIC" established by the American National Standard Institute (ANSI).

1

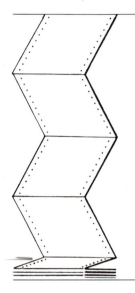

Inside the Computer

Overview

Suppose you wanted to improve on the power and usefulness of the pocket calculator that was discussed in the Introduction. As it stands now, you can answer simple questions like: "What is the unit cost of a 12-ounce jar of peanut butter that costs $1.03?" or "What is my gas mileage if I travel 250 miles on 12.5 gallons?" You can answer these questions by first figuring out your plan and then carrying out each step. For example, as suggested in the previous chapter, your steps for the unit price problem are to enter 103, press the divide key, enter 12, and press the equals key.

The pocket calculator is fine as long as your problems are fairly short and require very little information to be stored or displayed. However, suppose you wanted a listing of the unit price for all items in a store. What would you need to do to improve your calculator so it could handle larger and more problems? Let's try to answer this question by looking at each component in a computer system.

First, you need a way to give the computer a long list of instructions in a language that is like English. On your calculator you must enter each instruction, one step at a time, and it is carried out. Such a system is very tedious and requires your attention to each little step that the computer executes. The following is an example of a program for solving the unit price problem:

1. Put this number in memory space 1

2. *103*
3. *Put this number in memory space 2*
4. *12*
5. *Divide the number in space 1 by the number in space 2 and put the result in space 3*
6. *Display the number in memory space 3*
7. *That is all*

Thus we need a computer system that will accept a list of instructions all at once and will work out the answer on its own. In other words, instructing the computer with a program rather than pressing keys for each operation is a big advance.

But what modifications must we make to our calculator so that it can handle programs? Let's first consider the input component. We will need a way of reading entire programs and long lists of data; the keyboard of a calculator is just too limited. We need a full keyboard such as that of a typewriter so that we can write our instructions in an English-like language. A computer terminal with a full keyboard (or a card reader or a tape reader) will greatly expand the number and kind of instructions we can give the computer.

Now, let's consider the output device. The 10- or 12-digit readout on a calculator is just too small. We need to be able to display long lists of numbers or even words. To accommodate this need, we could expand the size of the screen so that 40 lines of 80 characters each can be displayed at once. Or we could use a printer as the output device so that large quantities of numbers and words could be printed out on paper. Thus, a TV-sized output screen or a printer is needed.

To store vast amounts of information we need more than the two memory spaces in our pocket calculator. In fact we may need hundreds or thousands or millions of memory spaces. Both memory added to the central processing unit and back-up memory are needed. Back-up memories that could be added to our system include magnetic tapes or disks.

Our calculator has only four arithmetic functions: addition, subtraction, multiplication, division. To accomplish more tasks we could add to these. We need a square root function, geometric functions, exponential functions, and many others; you may know that some sophisticated calculators do have more than just four functions. We also need some logical operations: the computer must be able to tell if one number is larger than another, for example. Thus the arithmetic/logic component must be improved.

Finally, what about the executive control component that forms the heart of the CPU? When you use a calculator, you are providing the executive control because you are the one who decides what to do next. However, if we have a program list like the one above, we need a computer system that can start at the top and execute each step in order. It must be able to tell which step it is on, when it has finished that step, and which step to carry out next. Thus we need an executive control component in our CPU. You may know that some calculators already have a primitive form of executive control; if you insert a sequence like ((5 + 3)/4) the calculator will first perform the addition (5 + 3 = 8) and then the division (8/4 = 2). In this case you specify the order of execution using parentheses. Thus the parentheses are a primitive kind of executive control allowed on some calculators.

In this chapter you will learn how each one of these expanded components of a computer system operates.

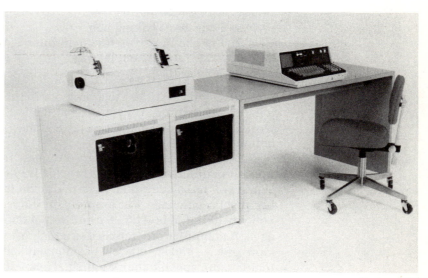

Courtesy of IBM

What Is a Program?

statement
program

A **statement** is an instruction that tells the computer to do something. A **program** is just a list of statements. Each statement in a program has its own line in the list. The computer will start at the statement at the top of the list and work its way down, doing one statement at a time, until it reaches the bottom of the list.

A program is much like a recipe. For example, consider the following recipe:

1. Take a bowl.
2. Put in 2 cups of flour.
3. Put in ½ cup of milk.
4. Put in 2 eggs.
5. Mix for 3 minutes.
6. Pour into a baking pan.
7. Put pan into oven for 20 minutes at 400 degrees.
8. Take out pan, and let cool.
9. That's all!

This recipe is similar to a program in the following ways: (1) it is a list of instructions; (2) you start at the top and work down; (3) you work on only one instruction at a time; (4) when you get to the bottom, you stop.

This recipe is also unlike a program in some ways. The most important difference is that this recipe is not as precise as a program. When you tell a computer what to do you must be very specific and use precise language. For example, in the recipe, step 1 does not tell you what kind of bowl to use and step 4 doesn't tell you to crack the eggs. A computer program is like a recipe, except that it uses a much more precise and specific set of statements. It uses a special language that is more specific than English. Thus you can think of a program as a recipe that is written in a very precise way and in a special language.

In this book you will learn how to use ten different BASIC statements, and you will learn what they mean in ordinary English. You can think of each BASIC statement as a kind of sentence that tells the computer to perform certain operations. BASIC statements can be put together in various ways into lists, with one statement per line; these lists are called programs because they tell the computer to perform a sequence of tasks in a certain order.

The Five Parts of a Computer

Computers vary greatly in size and structure and appearance. However, it is really not necessary to become an electronics expert to understand how to communicate with a computer. Therefore, this book will not emphasize the physical and electronic characteristics of computers but rather will focus on the main functions served by all computers. You will find that BASIC programming will be much easier to learn if you first take a few minutes to acquaint yourself with the five main functional parts of a computer.

Figure 6 represents the simple computer system that we will refer to in this book. Our computer is made up of five main parts:

Input Window. This allows communication from the outside world to the computer's memory.

Output Screen. This allows communication from the computer's memory back to the outside world.

Memory Scoreboard. This allows information to be stored in the computer.

Program List and Pointer Arrow. These tell the computer what to do and what order to go in.

Scratch Pad. This performs simple arithmetic operations and logical decisions.

Courtesy of IBM

Traditionally, these five functions have been called *input*, *output*, *memory*, *control*, and *logic*.

Input Window

input window

Notice that the **input window** in Figure 6 is divided into two parts, labeled "In" and "Finished." You can think of this as a ticket window. A line of cards with a number on each may be waiting outside. As the computer processes the number on each card, it brings that card through the window. When the computer needs to find the next data card, it takes the first card from those waiting outside the window; when it is done processing the card, it puts it in the finished pile.

Now, imagine a running computer. Before it begins to work, the numbers you are going to use must be lined up outside the "In" part of the input window. This is accomplished by using DATA or INPUT statements. When a number is moved from the outside of the window to the inside, the number is entered onto the memory scoreboard and then placed in the "Finished" part of the input window. This process is controlled by a READ statement.

Memory Scoreboard

A	A1	A2 17	...
B	B1	B2	...
C	C1	C2	...
D	D1	D2	...
E	E1	E2	...
F	F1	F2	...
G	G1	G2	...
H	H1	H2	...
J	J1	J2	...

Scratch Pad

$2 + 2 = 4$

Output Screen

Input Window

In   Finished

8 89 12 103

Pointer Arrow

Program List

1	Do this
2	Do that
3	Do this
4	Do that
5	Go to 1
6	Do this
7	Do that
8	Do this
9	Stop

Figure 6. *Inside a Computer System.*

Output Screen

output screen   The **output screen** pictured in Figure 6 can be thought of as a televi-
sion note pad for recording messages. This is where printed mes-
sages from the computer's memory to the outside world appear. Each
line on the screen is divided into five zones. When the computer
wants to print out a message it generally uses the next available zone
that is empty; if all the zones on a line are full it goes to the next line.
If all the lines are full it just erases the oldest line (on top) and pushes
all the messages up one line—this leaves a fresh new line at the
bottom for a new message. This is called *scrolling* because the output
screen acts like a scroll (see Figure 7). On some terminals, once the
screen is filled, a "screen full" condition is flashed, and the screen
must be erased before continuing.

Courtesy of Hewlett-Packard

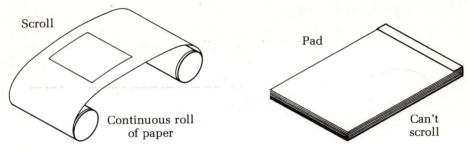

Scroll

Continuous roll
of paper

Pad

Can't
scroll

Figure 7.   Scrolling.

Writing a message on the output screen is the way in which the computer copies out a number or a word it has in its memory. This process is controlled by a PRINT statement.

Memory Scoreboard

memory scoreboard   Inside the computer is a large scoreboard called a **memory scoreboard.** Notice that it is divided into many spaces with room for one number or one message in each space (see Figure 6). Also note that each space is labeled with a name such as A1, B6, D2, and so on. **address**   These labels for each space are called addresses and each **address** always has some message (a number or written message) indicated in its space.

For example, there is a 17 in space A2. Imagine that the scoreboard is a chalkboard. To put a new number in space A2 you simply would erase the number 17, and the new number could be written instead. The number 2 could be added to the number in memory space A2, or it could be changed to zero. These processes are controlled by the LET, READ, and INPUT statements.

Program List and Pointer Arrow

Inside the computer is a place to put a list of things to do, called a **program list**   **program list,** and there is also a **pointer arrow,** which indicates what **pointer arrow**   step in the list the computer should work on. Each line in the program list has a number. When a program (i.e., a list of things to do) is inserted, the pointer arrow will point to the first line. When the first step of the program is completed (i.e., when the computer finishes whatever was written on the first line), the arrow will automatically move down to the next line, and so on down the list.

The pointer arrow will follow this procedure of pointing to the steps in order starting with the first line and going on down the list, unless it comes to a step that tells it to point to some other step; then it will point to that step and start working down from there. For example, the pointer may first point to the first line, then the computer will finish the first step and the arrow will shift to the second line, then the computer will finish that statement and the arrow will shift to the third line. The statement on the third line may say to move to the seventh line (skipping the fourth, fifth, and sixth lines) and so the arrow would move directly to the seventh line, then to the eighth, and so on. The control of the order of steps in the program list is done with GO TO, IF, FOR-NEXT, and END statements.

Scratch Pad

scratch pad

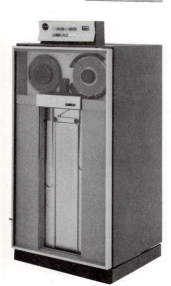

Courtesy of IBM

The fifth part of the computer is the **scratch pad;** this allows for temporary holding of numbers for arithmetic or logical operations. For example, if two numbers are to be added or subtracted or multiplied or divided, each will be temporarily written on the scratch pad and, when the answer is derived, it will be held temporarily on the scratch pad also. Similarly, if two numbers are to be compared based on some logical relationship such as determining if one is greater than the other, both numbers will be temporarily held on the scratch pad, and the result will also be temporarily held there.

Arithmetic operations are sometimes involved in LET or IF statements, and logical comparisons are involved in IF statements. Thus, you can think of the scratch pad as a place where arithmetic and logical answers are derived. Although the scratch pad has some small memory space for holding a few numbers, once an answer is found it is held only long enough for the computer to use it in the program; then all the calculations on the scratch pad are erased.

Courtesy of NCR Corporation

2

Reading and Writing

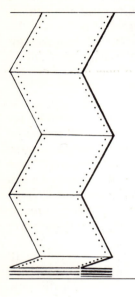

Overview

Let's suppose that you want to increase the power of your pocket calculator. You may want to use it to find the unit price of items in your grocery store, or to maintain a checkbook, or to do many other things. One modification that would be a big help would be to increase the number of memory spaces. Let's suppose you have a calculator that has two memories (indicated by separate memory entry and memory recall keys). How would you have to modify things if there were hundreds of memory spaces rather than just two?

First, let's look at how you get information into your new calculator. On a normal calculator you press the number keys on the keyboard, and then press a memory entry key to put the number into the calculator's memory. When you want to recall the number that is in that memory space you just press the memory recall key. But what happens when you have hundreds of memory spaces? You could have a separate memory entry and recall for each memory space, but that would add too many keys to your keyboard.

Fortunately, if you write your programs in BASIC, there are statements that will solve these problems. You use the DATA statement to tell the machine what numbers (or messages) you will put into the memory spaces; this is equivalent to pressing the number keys on the calculator (without pressing any entry key). The READ statement is used to tell the computer to place each particular number into a particular memory space; this is equivalent to pressing the memory entry key on the calculator. The PRINT statement is used to print out the contents of any memory space; this is equivalent to pressing the memory recall key on your calculator. Finally, the END statement is used to tell the computer that the program is over; it is similar to pressing the clear key on your calculator since it resets the machine and makes it ready to start a new task. Thus the DATA, READ, PRINT, and END statements allow you to start writing programs that read data into the computer and print data from the computer onto the output screen.

For example, suppose you wanted to find out the unit prices for products you were considering buying at a grocery store. One brand of peanut butter costs $1.03 for 12 ounces while another costs 66¢ for 7 ounces. If you had a calculator you could enter the price, then divide that number by the number of ounces in the product. A computer can be useful if you have many such computations to make. The following program shows how you might start to attack this problem:

```
10   READ T, N
20   DATA 103, 12
40   PRINT "TOTAL COST IS" T
60   PRINT "NUMBER OF OUNCES IS" N
99   END
```

This program will put 103 into memory space T and put 12 into memory space N. Then on the screen it will print the following:

```
TOTAL COST IS 103
NUMBER OF OUNCES IS 12
```

Then it will stop. Note that no computations have taken place; that will be covered in the next chapter. In this chapter you will learn about each of the four types of statements shown above. After reading this chapter you will be able to write and interpret simple programs involving these four statements.

READ and DATA Statements

The first two kinds of statements you will learn about in this chapter are READ and DATA. Look back at Figure 6 showing the five parts of the computer, and in particular look at the line of data cards waiting at the input window. How do these numbers get there and how is the order in the waiting line determined? The DATA statement is used to tell the computer which numbers are in line at the input window, and what order they are in.

When a data card is processed at the input window it is moved through the in window to the finished pile, and the number is stored in the computer's memory. How is this accomplished? The READ statement is used to tell the computer to take a number from the line waiting at the input window and to put that number in the computer's memory.

You should note that READ and DATA statements go together—whenever there is a READ statement the computer will also look for a DATA statement. These are the only two statements that relate to the input window part of the computer. (The INPUT statement, discussed in chapter 7, serves a related function.)

The format of the **READ statement** is

<table>
<tr><td>line
number
_____</td><td>READ</td><td>address
name
_____</td></tr>
</table>

where a line number goes into the blank on the left of READ and an address name goes into the blank on the right of READ. A line number is any whole number up to 5 digits (from 1 to 99999); statements in a program are carried out in the order of their line numbers. An address name is just a space in the computer's memory, and in BASIC there are many possible spaces. To store a number, each space that you use must be given a name consisting of a letter (A through Z) followed by a single digit (0 to 9) or just a letter alone (A through Z). Thus, you are now able to make up names for 286 memory spaces—26 spaces are labeled A through Z, plus 260 spaces are labeled by a letter followed by a digit. Each memory space may hold a number of any length (although the computer will round off extremely long numbers).

The format of the **DATA statement** is

<table>
<tr><td>line
number
_____</td><td>DATA</td><td>number
</td></tr>
</table>

where a line number goes into the first blank and the to-be-remembered number goes into the blank to the right of DATA. In BASIC, a number consists of digits, can have a minus sign (–) in front of it to indicate that it is a negative number, can have a decimal point (.), and can be in scientific notation (E).

It must be noted that the computer will first execute each of the DATA statements in a program, and then will go back to work on the other statements in order of their line numbers.

For example, suppose that the following two statements were in a larger program:

```
10   READ T
20   DATA 103
```

For the READ statement, the computer would be in the following state *before* it executes the READ statement:

▶ *There is a line of numbers (from the DATA statement) waiting at the input window, and there is some unknown number in memory space T. In this case, the number waiting at the input window is 103.*

For the READ statement, the computer would be in the following state *after* it executes the READ statement:

▶ *The top number from the data list will have moved through the input window and now be in the finished pile; thus, the line of numbers waiting at the input window will be reduced by one. The number that has just been processed at the input window will now be in memory space T. In this case, there will be no more numbers waiting at the input window, and the number 103 will now be in memory space T.*

For the statement

```
20   DATA 103
```

the computer will be in the following state *before* it executes the statement:

▶ *There are no numbers waiting at the input window (if this is the first DATA statement) or there are already some numbers waiting (if other DATA statements have already been executed before this one in the program). In this case, since there are no other DATA cards, there are no numbers waiting at the input window.*

After the statement is executed, the computer will be in the following state:

▶ *The number on the DATA card is now the last in line waiting at the input window. If there are no other DATA statements, the number 103 is now the only number waiting at the input window.*

The statement

```
10   READ T
```

means that the following operations will be performed:

1. Go to the line of numbers waiting at the input window and take the number that is first in line (e.g., 103 is waiting).
2. If there are no numbers waiting at the input window, print OUT OF DATA on the output screen and stop.
3. If there is a number, move it through the input window to the finished pile (e.g., move 103 to the finished pile).
4. Find the memory space labeled T.
5. Store the number from the input window in the memory space labeled T, destroying whatever previous number was stored there (e.g., put 103 in space T).
6. Go on to the next statement.

The operations performed for the statement

```
20 DATA 103
```

are as follows:

1. Place the number (103) in the line waiting at the input window behind any other numbers that may be waiting (e.g., put 103 at the input window as the first and only number in line).
2. Carry out any other required DATA statements.
3. Go on to the next statement in the program.

Note that DATA statements are carried out before READ statements so that the line of numbers waiting at the input window is ready. (You might remember that on our pocket calculator before any number could be stored in a memory cell, it had to be first entered on the keys.)

STYLE BOX: Line Numbers

line numbers

Remember that a program is just a list of statements, with one statement on each line. There are two important rules you must remember concerning **line numbers**:

1. Each line in the program list must have a unique line number (on the left).
2. A line number may be any integer from 1 to 99999.

error message

If any line on the program does not begin with a line number, an **error message** will be printed out on the output screen and the program will not run. If two lines have the same number, only the last one entered will be included.

The line numbers tell the computer how to order the statements. The program will be listed and executed in order, going from the line with the lowest line number to the line with the highest. Thus each line must have a unique line number. When a program is inserted into the program list space of the computer, the pointer arrow will point to the top line—that is, the line with the lowest line number; when it finishes it will go to the line with the second lowest number, and so on. For example, in the program given in the Overview, line 10 is first, then line 20, and so on.

There are also some helpful hints for using line numbers. Although these hints are not mandatory (as the two rules above are), they will help you write neat programs.

1. Do not number the lines of a program consecutively. Leave space such as going by 10's so that you can insert more statements later if you need to. (See the example in the Overview.)
2. Make all the line numbers in a program of equal length (e.g., all two-digit or all three-digit numbers) so that it will be easier for you to read your program. (See the example in the Overview.)

STYLE BOX: Address Names

address names

Both READ statements and PRINT statements use **address names.** In addition, many of the other statements you will learn about use address names. An address name is just a space in the computer's memory. In this book we will assume there are at least 286 spaces (although we can add more to this if needed). Each address name may contain just one number (of any length). The rules for making an address name for holding a number are as follows:

1. An address consists of one capital letter, such as A through Z.
2. Or an address consists of one capital letter followed by one digit.

Thus for any letter there are 11 names that can be used (A, A1, A2, A3, A4, A5, A6, A7, A8, A9, A0). Each refers to a unique memory space.

If you use a memory name that is not legal, the computer will print out an error message on the output screen and your program will not run. For example, which of the following are allowable memory addresses?

1A   12   AGE   AA   9Z   AL

You should have noticed that none of the above is allowable. The first one, 1A, and the fifth one, 9Z, begin with a number instead of a letter. The second one, 12, is not allowed because it has two digits instead of one (although later you will learn how to expand memory). The AGE, AA, and AL labels are not legal because they have more than one letter. Another common error is to mix up the number zero (0) and the letter O, or to mix up the number 1 and the letter l.

STYLE BOX: Numbers

number

Remember that any **number** can go into a memory space. A number has the following characteristics:

1. A number consists of any number of digits.
2. There may be a decimal point (.).
3. There may be a negative sign (—) to the left of the number.
4. There may be an E to express scientific notation.

In programming, it is important to note that numbers *do not* have commas or fractions (except as expressed as decimals) or signs of arithmetic operations.

If you use an illegal number, the computer will print out an error message on the output screen and the program will not run. For example, which of the following are legal numbers?

—.0096   99.88888   1,000,000   53½   12E2   12E—2   25²

You should note that the first number is legal since it consists only of digits and a minus sign and a decimal point. The second number is long, but it is also legal. The third number is not legal since it contains commas. The fourth is not legal since it has a fraction; if it said 53.5 it would be legal. The next two numbers are in scientific notation and are legal; translated, 12E2 is 12×10^2 or 1200, and 12E-2 is 12×10^{-2} or .12. Finally, the last number is not legal since it involves an arithmetic operation.

TRY IT

Suppose that two lines of a program were

```
10   READ Y
45   DATA -6
```

Assume there are no other READ or DATA statements in the program. List each operation that the computer would perform:

1. _____
2. _____
3. _____
4. _____
5. _____
6. _____

What number is in space Y after these two statements are performed?

_____ What number was in space Y before they were performed?

_____

Although you may have written your answer using different words, your operations should correspond with these:

1. Place the number 6 in the first spot in line waiting at the input window. (There are no other numbers there.)
2. Take the first number in line at the input window (6).
3. Move it through the window to the finished pile, thus leaving no numbers waiting at the window.
4. Find the memory space labeled Y.
5. Put the number 6 into the memory space Y, erasing whatever was there before.
6. Go on to the next statement.

A common error is to forget step 3; this leaves the number 6 still in line and gives the computer no way to go on to other numbers. Before the statements are performed, an unknown number is in space Y. After they are performed, −b is in space Y.

TRY IT

Suppose you wanted to get the number 8.99 into memory space T1. How could you do that using a READ and DATA statement? Fill in your answer below:

_____   READ   _____
_____   DATA   _____

Although you may have used *any* legal line number, your answer should look something like the following:

```
10   READ T1
20   DATA 8.99
```

A common error is to say:

```
10   READ 8.99
```

The problem with this is that the computer has no way of knowing which memory space should be used to hold the number.

More About READ and DATA Statements

You now know how to tell the computer to read in a single number from a DATA statement into a particular memory space. Suppose you wanted to read in several different numbers, each into a separate memory space? For example, in the unit price problem you must read in the total cost and the number of ounces. You could write a long list of individual READ and DATA statements, or you could use a shorter technique as shown below. The format for the READ statement is

where a line number goes in the blank to the left of READ, and different address names go into each blank to the right of READ. The list of address names may be one, two, three, four, or more but each name must be separated by commas. (The length of the list is limited by the size of the computer's memory.)

The format for DATA statements is

where a line number goes in the blank to the left of DATA and numbers go into each of the other blanks. The list of numbers can have one, two, three, four, or more numbers, but each number must be separated by a comma.

STYLE BOX: Spacing

When you write a statement on a line, you may wonder how many spaces to use to separate the parts of the statement. You should know that, as far as the computer is concerned, it doesn't matter. Although some computers treat blanks in numbers or line numbers as zeros, the general rule about spacing is as follows:

▶ *The computer ignores blank spaces.*

Thus as far as the computer is concerned, the statement

```
10   READ A, B
```

is exactly the same thing as

```
10   READA,B
```

However, there are some helpful hints that will allow you to write programs that *you* can read:

1. Always leave one or two spaces after the line number.
2. Try to space READ and DATA statements the same way.
3. Indent parts of the program that are in loops. (See Chapters 5 and 6.)

For example, suppose that the following two statements were in a larger program:

```
10   READ T,   N
20   DATA 103, 12
```

For the statement

```
10   READ T, N
```

the computer would be in the following state *before* it executes the statement:

▶ *There is a list of numbers (in this case the numbers are 103 and 12) waiting at the input window, and there are unknown numbers in memory spaces T and N.*

After this statement is executed, the computer will be in the following state:

▶ *The two numbers from the data list (103 and 12) are now in the finished pile, there are no numbers waiting at the input window, memory space T has 103 in it, and memory space N has 12 in it.*

For the statement

```
20   DATA 103, 12
```

the computer will be in the following state before it executes this statement:

▶ *There are no numbers waiting at the input window (assuming this is the only DATA statement in the program).*

After this statement is executed, the computer will be in the following state:

▶ *The two numbers from the DATA statement are now in the line waiting at the input window. If this is the only DATA card, then numbers will be waiting at the window in the order 103 first and 12 next.*

The statement

```
10 READ T, N
```

means that the following operations will be performed:

1. Go to the pile of data cards that are waiting at the input window and take the first two numbers in line (i.e., 103 and 12).
2. If there are not enough numbers waiting at the input window, carry out steps 3, 4, and 5 for the numbers that are waiting, print "OUT OF DATA," and then stop.
3. If there are enough numbers, move the numbers through the input window to the finished pile.
4. Find the memory space corresponding to T and N.
5. Store the first number in T and the second number in N, destroying whatever numbers were previously stored there.
6. Go on to the next statement.

The operations performed for the statement

```
20   DATA 103, 12
```

are as follows:

1. Place the numbers 103 and 12 in line waiting at the input window, in that order, and behind any other numbers that may be waiting. (If this is the only DATA statement, then the numbers waiting at the window will be 103 and 12, in that order).
2. Carry out any other DATA statements.

3. If there are no other DATA statements, go on to the next statement in the program.

TRY IT

Suppose the following two lines were in a program:

```
30   READ   T,   Y,Q,  X
60   DATA 35, -6.6,  13E2
```

Assume there are no other READ or DATA statements in the program. List the operations that the computer would perform:

1. _____

2. _____

3. _____

4. _____

5. _____

Although you may have written your answer in a different form, your operations should correspond to the following:

1. Place the numbers 35, −6.6, and 13E2 in line at the input window so that 35 is first and 13E2 last.
2. Go to the pile of data numbers waiting at the input window and take the first four in line.
3. Find the memory spaces labeled T, Y, Q, and X.
4. Put 35 into T, put −6.6 into Y, and put 13E2 into Q, destroying whatever was in each space previously.
5. Since there is no number for X, leave that location as is, print "OUT OF DATA," and stop the program.

A common error is to omit step 5—since there is not enough data to fill the memory spaces, the computer must stop.

TRY IT

Suppose you wanted to put the number 1 into space A, 2 into B, 3 into C, and 4 into D. Write a program, using a single READ and a single DATA statement.

```
_____    READ    _____
_____    DATA    _____
```

Although your line numbers may be different, your two statements should look like the following:

```
 5 READ A, B, C, D
10 DATA 1, 2, 3, 4
```

You might note that the following is an equivalent way to accomplish the same goal:

```
 5 READ D, C, B, A
10 DATA 4, 3, 2, 1
```

A common error is to leave out a comma. Thus "DATA 4 3 2 1" would be read by the computer as presenting one single number: four thousand, three hundred and twenty one.

PRINT Statements

Now that you know how to get information from the outside world into the computer's memory, let's look at a way of getting the computer to write out what is in its memory for the outside world. Remember the output screen in Figure 6; it's one of the five parts of the computer. The **PRINT statement** provides a way of getting the computer to write a message on a line of the output screen. If a program contains no PRINT statement, there will be no way for the computer to show you what it has done. Outputting is accomplished by using

<u>line</u>   <u>address</u>
number   PRINT name

where a line number goes in the space before the PRINT and an address name goes in the space after the PRINT. An address name is just a space in the computer's memory; it is labeled by a single letter or a letter followed by a single digit.

The PRINT statement tells the computer to print out the number it is storing in a particular memory space, but the number is still kept in memory, too. When the computer prints out a number from a memory space, that memory is still retained; in essence, a copy of the contents of the memory space is produced, without disturbing the original. However, when the computer reads in a number into a memory space any previous number is destroyed. This difference between READing and PRINTing is called **destructive read-in** and **nondestructive read-out.** The memory scoreboard is not altered by a PRINT statement but is altered by a READ statement.

destructive read-in
nondestructive
read-out

For example, the statement

```
40 PRINT T
```

means that the following condition exists in the computer before the statement is executed:

▶ *There is a number stored in memory space T.*

After this statement is executed, the computer is in the following state.

▶ *The number is still in memory space T, the number has been printed out on the next available space on the output screen, and the computer has gone on to work on the next statement. (If no number has been stored in T, the computer may give you an error message or may print out some default value such as zero.)*

The operations performed for the statement

```
40   PRINT T
```

are as follows:

1. Check to see what number is stored in memory space T, leaving that number unchanged.
2. Print out that number on the next available space on the output screen.
3. Move on to the next statement.

TRY IT

Suppose that you know that there is a number 55 in memory space A, a number 66 in memory space B, and a 77 in space C. Suppose that the computer comes to the following lines in a program:

```
50   PRINT A
55   PRINT A
60   PRINT C
65   PRINT B
```

What will the output of these lines look like on the output screen? _____ What numbers will be in memory spaces A, B, and C after these four statements are executed? A _____, B _____, C _____

The output will consist of one number on each line of the output screen as follows:

```
55
55
77
66
```

The memory spaces are not altered so that A still has 55, B has 66, and C has 77.

TRY IT

Suppose there was some number in space Q3 and you wanted to know what it was. The statement to solve this problem is

_____   PRINT   _____

The answer is

    50   PRINT Q3

where any number could be the line number.

More About PRINT Statements

Now you know how to have the computer tell you what it knows by asking for one memory space at a time. However, in the unit price problem, you may want several values printed out. If you want to find out what is in several memory spaces, you may use the format

line number	PRINT	address name	,	address name	,	address name
_____		_____		_____		_____

where a line number goes to the left of PRINT and address names go to the right of PRINT. Any number of address names may be used, but they must be separated by commas.

For example, the statement

    40   PRINT T, N

means that the following conditions exist in the computer before the statement is executed:

▶ *There is a number in each of the memory spaces listed above.*

After this statement is executed, the computer is in the following condition:

▶ *The same numbers are still in each of the memory spaces, two numbers have been printed out on the next two available spaces of the output screen, and the computer has gone on to the next statement.*

The statement

    40   PRINT T, N

means that the following operations will be performed:

1. Check to see what numbers are in the T and N memory spaces, leaving them unchanged.

2. Print out those two numbers in the next two available spaces on the output sheet, with one number in T first and the other number in N last.
3. Go on to the next statement.

TRY IT

Suppose the computer comes to the following statement:

    50   PRINT A1, B1

List each of the operations that the computer would perform, assuming A1 has a 5 and B1 has a 10 in it.

1. _____

2. _____

3. _____

Your answer should have the following ideas in it:

1. Check to see what number is in A1 and what number is in B1, but do not alter them.
2. Print the number from A1 (this is a 5) in the first available space on the output screen, and then print the number from B1 (this is a 10) in the next available space on the output screen.
3. Go on to the next statement.

TRY IT

Suppose you know that a 5 is in memory space R, a 78 in memory space S, and a 32 in memory space T. How could you get the computer to print out 32 and 5 and 78 in that order by using just one PRINT statement?

    _____   PRINT   _____

The answer could have any line number, but should look like this:

    60   PRINT T, R, S

A common error is to put letters in the wrong order; for example, if the address labels were in the order R, S, T, then the numbers printed would be in the order 5, 78, 32.

PRINT Statements with Messages

The PRINT statement may also be used to have the computer write out words or any alphanumeric strings. This is helpful in reminding you what is being printed. The format of the expanded PRINT statement is

line number	PRINT	"message"	address name	address name	address name
_____		_____	_____ ,	_____ ,	_____

message   where a line number goes in the first blank, any **message** can go in between the quotation marks, and any address names may follow. It is also possible to have no address names following the message.

For example, the statement

```
30   PRINT "TOTAL COST IS" T
```

means that before this statement the computer is in the following state:

▶ *A number is in space T.*

After this statement, the following is the case:

▶ *There is still the same number in space T, and on the output screen appears "TOTAL COST IS 103" (if the number in T is 103).*

The operations for

```
30   PRINT "TOTAL COST IS" T
```

are as follows:

1. Go to next line of output screen and print TOTAL COST IS.
2. Find number in memory space T but do not alter it.
3. Print that number in next space on the output screen.
4. Go on to next statement.

As another example, consider this statement:

```
30   PRINT "THIS GIVES UNIT PRICES"
```

The conditions in the computer before this statement are that the computer has just been directed to line 30. The conditions afterward are that the next line of the output screen has this message:

THIS GIVES UNIT PRICES.

The operations involved for the statement

    30   PRINT "THIS GIVES UNIT PRICES"

are the following:

1. Go to the next clean line of the output screen and write THIS GIVES UNIT PRICES.
2. Go on to the next statement.

TRY IT

Suppose the only print statement in a given program is

    90   PRINT "A1, A2, A3"

What will the computer do when it comes to this statement?

1. _____

2. _____

3. _____

4. _____

The following operations will be performed:

1. The computer will find the next space on the output screen.
2. The computer will print out the message inside the quotation marks exactly as it is written: A1, A2, A3.
3. The computer will go on to the next statement.

The computer will not examine memory spaces A1, A2, or A3 since these were enclosed in quotation marks. However, if the PRINT statement had said

    90   PRINT A1, A2, A3

the computer would perform the following:

1. Find the next spaces on the output screen.
2. Find the numbers in A1, A2, A3, but do not alter them.
3. Print out these numbers in the next three spaces on the output screen.
4. Go on to the next statement.

Thus these examples show why you must be careful about how you use quotation marks.

TRY IT

Suppose that you know the number 5 is memory space R. Write a program that will result in the following message being printed on the output screen: THE ANSWER IS 5.

```
_____    PRINT    _____

_____
```

There are several ways to get this output. One very simple way is to say

```
20   PRINT "THE ANSWER IS 5"
```

The computer will simply print out the message inside the quotation marks. But, although the output produced is the one desired, it does not do what the problem asked, namely to use the fact that 5 is in R. Another statement uses the memory space R:

```
20   PRINT "THE ANSWER IS" R
```

In this case the computer will print out the message inside the quotation marks followed by whatever number is in space R—in this case 5.

END Statement

The last kind of statement you will learn about in this chapter is the **END statement;** this shows that the program is over. Look back at Figure 6 showing the parts of the computer, and in particular look at the list of things to do in the program list. The computer will stop when it comes to the end of the list. The END statement is used simply to announce that the end of the program has come. Whenever the computer is given a program, it will expect that the last line of the program will be END. If you forgot to use the END statement, the program may still run but an error message may be printed on the output screen. The format is

```
line
number
_____    END
```

where a line number goes in the blank.
    For example, the statement

```
99   END
```

means that the computer is in the following state before this statement is executed:

▶ *The computer has just finished the statement above the END statement or been directed to go to this line.*

After the statement is executed, the computer is in the following state:

▶ *The computer is finished with this program and is ready for a new one.*

The operations performed for the statement

99 END

are as follows:

1. The end of this program has come, so stop working on it.
2. Print READY and be prepared to respond to further instructions.

TRY IT

Suppose a program ended with two END statements:

90   END
91   END

What would the computer do?

_____

_____

_____

_____

_____

When the computer came to the first END statement, it would stop working on the program and look for the next program to work on. Thus the second END statement would be ignored! (If the program had the statement

40   IF X = 5 THEN 91

the first END would be bypassed.) It is important to give the END statement a high line number, in case you decide to add more statements to your program.

PROGRAM QUIZ

You have now learned enough to write simple programs. In this chapter you have learned about four important BASIC statements: READ, DATA, PRINT, and END. In this section you will be given some practice in putting these four statements together into actual programs. It is important that you fully understand each statement, so you should go back and restudy any statements you don't yet understand before you try this section. Also, you may have noticed that this book emphasizes practice in interpreting what a statement or program will do just as much as practice in writing programs. This is done because most programmers agree that the most time-consuming part of programming is "debugging"—finding the errors in a program that does not run by interpreting what it does.

(1) Consider the following program:

```
10   READ X
20   READ Y
30   DATA 5
40   DATA 10
50   PRINT X
60   PRINT Y
70   END
```

What will be the output of this program? _____
In a sentence, tell what the computer does. _____
List each operation the computer will perform:

_____

_____

_____

_____

_____

_____

This program will print out the number 5 and then the number 10 on the output screen. The job that this program accomplishes is to read in two numbers into memory and print out those two numbers. The operations for this program are as follows:

    1. The number 5 is put first in line at the input window.
    2. The number 10 is put second in line at the input window.

3. The first number (5) is moved through the window to the finished pile.
4. Memory space X is found, and the number that was just processed (5) is put into space X, erasing previous numbers in X.
5. The next number in line (10) is moved through the input window to the finished pile.
6. Memory space Y is found, and the number that was just processed (10) is put into space Y, erasing whatever was there before.
7. The number in memory space X is found and printed on the first available line on the output screen.
8. The number in memory space Y is found and printed on the next line after that on the output screen.
9. The program is over, so the computer waits for new directions.

(2) Modify the following program so that you use only one READ, one DATA, and one PRINT statement.

```
10    READ X
20    READ Y
30    DATA 5
40    DATA 10
50    PRINT X
60    PRINT Y
70    END
```

_____

_____

_____

_____

_____

Below are two ways to accomplish this goal:

```
10    READ X, Y        10    DATA 5, 10
20    DATA 5, 10       20    READ X, Y
30    PRINT X, Y       30    PRINT X, Y
40    END              40    END
```

Note that DATA need not follow READ but that PRINT must follow READ.

(3) Write a program to print out the numbers 1, 2, 3, 4, 5, 6, 7, 8, 9, 10.

_____

_____

_____

_____

_____

_____

One way to accomplish this is

```
10   PRINT "1, 2, 3, 4, 5, 6, 7, 8, 9, 10"
20   END
```

Another way is

```
10   READ X1, X2, X3, X4, X5, X6, X7, X8, X9, X0
20   DATA 1, 2, 3, 4, 5, 6, 7, 8, 9, 10
30   PRINT X1, X2, X3, X4, X5, X6, X7, X8, X9, X0
40   END
```

(4) Write a program to read in four numbers (1, 2, 3, 4), then print them out in order, and then print them out in reverse order.

_____

_____

_____

_____

_____

_____

One way to solve this problem is

```
10   READ A, B, C, D
20   DATA 1, 2, 3, 4
30   PRINT A, B, C, D
40   PRINT D, C, B, A
50   END
```

(5) What will be the output of the following program? _____
  What problem will the program solve? _____

```
10   READ X, X, X, X
20   DATA 5, 10, 15, 20
30   PRINT X, X, X, X
40   END
```

The output will be 20 printed four times on the output screen. This program first reads in a 5, erases that and inserts a 10, then erases that for a 15, and then erases that for a 20. Then when the computer is told to print X it will write 20. This program *might* have been intended to read in four numbers and print them out; however, it fails to do this because only one memory space is used. Each time a number is read into X the number read just before is erased.

(6) Modify the following program so that it prints out all four data numbers.

```
10   READ X, X, X, X
20   DATA 5, 10, 15, 20
30   PRINT X, X, X, X
40   END
```

The modified program could be

```
10   READ X1, X2, X3, X4
20   DATA 5, 10, 15, 20
30   PRINT X1, X2, X3, X4
40   END
```

Summary

So far this chapter has analyzed each of four BASIC statements that are required to solve the unit price problem. First, you learned how to use each statement. This is like learning to bake by first learning how to crack eggs, then learning how to use a mixer, then learning how to add seasoning, etc. Your second major task is to learn how to put the statements together to form a program that will solve your problem. Can you see how the statements

```
10   READ T, N
20   DATA 103, 12
40   PRINT "TOTAL COST IS" T
60   PRINT "NUMBER OF OUNCES IS" N
99   END
```

will accomplish the job of putting 103 into space T, 12 into space N, and then printing out two messages on the output screen?

Let's look at another example that is a bit different than the unit price problem. Suppose you were a teacher who wanted to keep a computerized gradebook. Suppose one student, Sam, has received scores of 95, 85, and 75 on three exams. You would like to record these scores and calculate the average. Based on the kinds of BASIC statements you have learned so far, what would you do? One approach to this problem is as follows:

```
10   READ E1, E2, E3
20   DATA 95, 85, 75
40   PRINT "FOR SAM"
60   PRINT "EXAM 1 SCORE IS" E1
70   PRINT "EXAM 2 SCORE IS" E2
80   PRINT "EXAM 3 SCORE IS" E3
99   END
```

This program would instruct the computer to put 95 into space E1, 85 into space E2, and 75 into space E3. Then it would print the following on the screen:

```
FOR SAM
EXAM 1 SCORE IS 95
EXAM 2 SCORE IS 85
EXAM 3 SCORE IS 75
```

Note that this program does not calculate the average of the three scores. In the following chapters you will see how to build on this program by using new kinds of statements.

3

Arithmetic

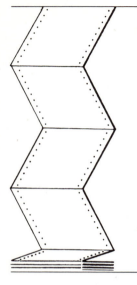

Overview

In the previous chapter you learned how to get information into memory spaces and how to get it out of memory spaces. The four kinds of statements you learned are necessary because we have greatly increased the number of memory spaces in our computer.

Remember that your pocket calculator can perform arithmetic computations using addition, subtraction, multiplication, and division. You simply enter the first number, then indicate the operation, then enter the second number, and then press the equals key. Your answer will appear on the screen. However, suppose you want to make computations in a computer that has many memory spaces. One way might be to recall one memory, then indicate the operation, then recall another memory, then store the answer in another memory space. All of these operations would take many steps on your calculator, but they are accomplished by just one statement in BASIC—the LET statement. (Some versions of BASIC allow you to make computations using the PRINT statement, such as PRINT (103/12) or PRINT T/N. This shortcut will be described in Chapter 9.)

In this chapter you will add the LET statement to your growing repertoire. The LET statement allows you to do arithmetic. Thus in the preceding chapter you learned about reading and writing; now you will learn about the third "R," arithmetic.

The LET statement will help complete our unit price program. The program below shows how you could find the unit price for a 12-ounce jar of peanut butter costing $1.03.

```
10   READ T, N
20   DATA 103, 12
30   LET U = T/N
40   PRINT "TOTAL COST IS" T
60   PRINT "NUMBER OF OUNCES IS" N
80   PRINT "UNIT COST IS" U
99   END
```

This program adds two lines (line 30 and line 80) to the program given in the Overview of the preceding chapter. This program will put 103 into memory space T and 12 into memory space N. Then it will divide the number in T by the number in N and put the result in memory space U. In this case the result is 8.5833333. On the screen it will then print the following three lines:

```
TOTAL COST IS 103
NUMBER OF OUNCES IS 12
UNIT COST IS 8.5833333
```

Then the program is finished. Note that you need a new program for each unit price you compute. After reading this chapter you will be able to write programs that involve such computations.

Three Kinds of LET Statements

The **LET statement** allows you to change the contents of a memory space. This is similar to using the memory entry key on a calculator because it allows you to put a new number in the memory space. The LET statement is confusing to many students until they see that it really can be used in three different ways:

Counter Set LET. This allows you to assign a number to a memory space (in the memory scoreboard). This is like entering a number into one of the memories of a pocket calculator; to get 103 into memory space 1, for example, you would press 103 in the number keyboard, then press the memory 1 enter key. All this is accomplished in BASIC by a Counter Set LET statement, such as: 10 LET T = 103.

Arithmetic LET. This allows you to perform some arithmetic computations on numbers and store the answer in a particular memory space (in the memory scoreboard). This is like performing a calculation on your calculator and then storing the answer in a memory space; for example, you could press 103 in the keyboard, then the divide key, then 12 in the keyboard, then the equals key (this gives a result of 8.5833333), and then press the memory 1 enter key (to store this result). All of these operations are accomplished in BASIC by an Arithmetic LET statement, such as: 30 LET U = 103/12.

Formula LET. This allows you to express some algebraic equation so that when values are plugged into it, an answer is calculated, and the answer is stored at a particular memory space (in the memory scoreboard). This is like performing a calculation on our pocket calculator that uses a number from a memory space and then stores the answer in a memory space. For example, you could press memory 1 recall (this brings up 103, let's say), then the divide key, then memory 2 recall (this contains 12, let's say), then the equals key (this results in an answer of 8.5833333), and then press the memory 1 enter key (this puts the answer in memory space 1). All of these operations would be carried out by a Formula LET statement, such as: 30 LET U = T/N.

To understand LET statements, first think about some of the parts of the computer you have learned about—in particular, remember the memory scoreboard and the scratch pad. The LET statement allows you to change the contents of a space (or spaces) in the memory scoreboard. In addition, some LET statements involve arithmetic operations that are performed in the scratch pad before the result is stored in a space on the memory scoreboard.

Counter Set LET

To set an address name to a certain value, LET can be used as a **Counter Set LET statement.** The format is

line
number _____   LET   address
name _____   =   number or
address name _____

where a line number goes into the first blank, an address name goes in the blank on the right side of LET, and a number or another address name goes in the blank to the right of the equals sign.

For example, the statement

    30   LET T = 103

means that before this statement is executed the computer is in the following state:

▶ *Some unknown number is being stored in space T.*

After this statement has been executed, the computer is in the following state:

▶ *The number 103 is now stored in memory space T instead of whatever was there before, and the computer has gone on to the next statement.*

The statement

    30   LET T = 103

means that the following operations will be performed:

1. Find memory space T.
2. Destroy the number in memory space T.
3. Put 103 in that space instead.
4. Go on to the next statement.

Another example is the statement

    30   LET T = T1

This means that before this statement, the computer is in the following state:

▶ *Some number is stored in memory space T and some number is stored in memory space T1.*

After this statement is executed, the computer is in the following state:

▶ *The original number is still in space T1, and it is also stored in T (instead of whatever was there before), and the computer is working on the next statement.*

The operations performed for the statement

    30   LET T = T1

are as follows:

1. Find memory spaces T and T1.
2. Destroy whatever number was stored in memory space T.
3. See the number that is stored in space T1 but do not destroy it.
4. Put that number in memory space T.
5. Move on to the next statement.

TRY IT

Write a LET statement to get the number 5 into memory space X.

    _____   LET   _____

Your answer should look something like this:

    100   LET X = 5

A common error is to reverse the equals sign:

    100   LET 5 = X

Remember that the computer will try to take the value on the right and put it into the memory space indicated on the left of the equals sign; here, this will result in an error message (because 5 is not an address name but a number).

TRY IT

Can you think of an equivalent way to get the number 5 into memory space X, without using a LET statement?

Your answer could be the following:

```
5    READ X
10   DATA 5
```

These two statements accomplish the same task as

```
10   LET X = 5
```

because they both end up with a number 5 being put into space X.

TRY IT

List the operations performed by the computer for the following statement. Assume that before this statement is executed there is a 16 in memory space A1 and a 2 in memory space A2.

```
10   LET A1 = A2
```

The operations are as follows:

1. _____

2. _____

3. _____

4. _____

5. _____

Also, the number in space A1 after this statement is executed is _____ and the number in space A2 is _____.

Your answer should list the following operations:

1. Find memory space A1 and find memory space A2.
2. Destroy the number in A1.
3. Find the number in A2 but do not destroy it.
4. Put that number also in space A1.
5. Move on to the next statement.

Although your operations may not be expressed in exactly this form, you should have mentioned each of these steps. Also, the number in A1 will be 2 and the number in A2 will be 2 after this statement is executed.

Arithmetic LET

A second function of the LET statement is to perform a computation on some numbers and then put the answer in a memory space. The format of the **Arithmetic LET statement** is

line
number ___ LET address
name ___ = number ___ operation number ___

where a line number goes in the blank on the left of LET, an address name goes in the first blank on the right of LET, the first blank to the right of the equals sign is a number, the second blank to the right of the equals sign is an operation sign (either addition, subtraction, multiplication, division, or exponentiation), and the third blank to the right of the equals is a number. The five arithmetic operations are symbolized as follows: + means *add*, − means *subtract*, * means *multiply*, / means *divide*, and ↑ means *raise to a power*.

For example, the statement

```
30   LET U = 103/12
```

means that before this statement is executed the computer is in the following state:

▶ *Some unknown value is in memory space U and the answer to 103 divided by 12 has not been determined.*

After the statement has been executed, the computer is in the following state:

▶ *The number 8.5833333 is now in memory space U instead of whatever was previously there, and the computer has gone on to the next statement.*

For the statement

```
30   LET U = 103/12
```

the following operations must be performed:

1. Find memory space U.
2. Destroy the number stored in memory space U.
3. Perform the computation 103/12.
4. Place the answer (8.5833333) in memory space U.
5. Go on to the next statement.

Longer chains of computations may be specified by the Arithmetic LET statement, such as:

```
30   LET U = (100 + 3)/(10 + 2)
```

Before this statement:

▶ *There is some number in memory space U.*

After this statement:

▶ *The number in memory space U is 8.5833333.*

The operations performed for the statement

```
30   LET U = (100 + 3)/(10 + 2)
```

are as follows:

1. Find memory space U.
2. Destroy whatever number is in it.
3. Add 100 plus 3, add 10 plus 2, and then divide the first result by the second.
4. Put that number (8.5833333) into memory space U.
5. Go on to the next statement.

STYLE BOX: The Five Arithmetic Symbols

LET statements allow you to perform arithmetic operations. The five operations that the computer can perform require the following symbols:

+ means *add*, just as X + Y means *add* X *and* Y
− means *subtract*, just as X − Y means *subtract* Y *from* X
* means *multiply*, just as X * Y means *multiply* X *times* Y
/ means *divide*, just as X/Y means *divide* X *by* Y
↑ means *raise to a power*, just as X ↑ Y means *raise* X *to the* Y *power*

(In some systems, X**Y or X'Y mean "raise X to the Y power.") For examples, consider these problems:

5 + 2 = _____
5 − 2 = _____
5 * 2 = _____
5 / 2 = _____
5 ↑ 2 = _____

The answers are 7, 3, 10, 2.5, and 25, respectively.

STYLE BOX: Formula Writing

In using LET statements you must be careful to note that the equals sign (=) does not really mean "equals"! The real definition is

> ▶ Take the number from the right of the equals sign and put it in the memory space indicated on the left of the equals sign.

Thus the statement

    10   LET A5 = A6

does not mean the same thing as

    10   LET A6 = A5

The first statement means that the number in A6 will also be placed in A5. The second means that the number in A5 will also be placed in A6. Thus if a 5 is in A5 and a 6 is in A6 before these statements, then the first statement would result in both having a 6 while the second would result in both having a 5.

Also be careful not to confuse the statement

    10   LET X = Y + 5

with a statement like

    10   LET Y + 5 = X

The first one is perfectly legal but the second is not. The item to the left of the equals sign must be one address name—the one that is going to be changed.

TRY IT

Suppose that the computer comes to a statement

    20   LET N = 5 - 2 * (2 ' 3)

What number will be in memory space N after this statement is executed? _____ What operations does the computer perform?

1. _____

2. _____

3. _____

4. _____

5. _____

The number in N will be −11. The computer arrives at this in the following way:

1. Find memory space N.
2. Erase value in N.
3. Raise 2 to the third power ($2 \times 2 \times 2 = 8$); then multiply that by 2 ($2 \times 8 = 16$); then subtract that from 5 ($5 - 16 = -11$).
4. Put that number (-11) into space N.
5. Go on to the next statement.

TRY IT

Suppose that you want to find out the value of 666×6666 and store the answer in memory space K. Write a LET statement to accomplish this.

_____   LET   _____

One answer could be the following:

```
45  LET K = 666 * 6666
```

Formula LET

The third type of LET statement can be called a **Formula LET statement**; its format is

line number	LET	address name	=	number or address name	operation	number or address name
_____		_____		_____	_____	_____

where a line number goes in the blank to the left of LET and an address name goes in the blank just to the right of LET; then either an address name or a number goes in the first blank to the right of the equals sign, an arithmetic operation sign goes in the second blank after the equals sign, and either an address name or a number goes in the third blank after the equals sign.

For example, the statement

```
30  LET U = T/N
```

means that the computer is in the following state before this statement:

▶ *There are numbers stored in memory space U, T and N.*

After the statement is executed, the computer is in the following state:

▶ *There is a new number in memory space U that is equal to the value stored in T divided by the value in N. (E.g., if T had contained a 103 and N had 12 before the statement was executed, U would now contain a 8.5833333.) Also, the computer has gone on to the next statement.*

The operations involved for the statement

```
30   LET U = T/N
```

are as follows:

1. Find memory spaces U, T, and N.
2. Check the numbers in T and N but do not alter them.
3. Divide the number from space T by the number in space N.
4. Erase the original number from U.
5. Insert the new answer in memory space U.
6. Go on to the next statement.

As another example, consider the statement

```
90   LET C = C + 1
```

Before this statement is executed, the computer is in the following state:

▶ *Some number is stored in memory space C.*

After this statement is executed, the computer is in the following state:

▶ *The number that is in C is equal to the original number plus 1, and the computer is working on the next statement.*

The statement

```
90   LET C = C + 1
```

means that the following operations are performed:

1. Find memory space C.
2. Add 1 to the value in C.
3. Now destroy whatever number was stored at C.
4. Put the new sum in C instead.
5. Move on to the next statement.

STYLE BOX: Chains of Arithmetic

You may ask the computer to perform a chain of operations in a LET statement. All the operations must be on a single line.

For example, the expression

$$\frac{X + Y}{Z}$$

would be written as

(X + Y)/Z

When there is more than one operation to be performed on a line, the computer will move from right to left except for the following rules:

1. All expressions with ↑ will be calculated first.
2. All expressions with * or / will be calculated next.
3. All expressions with + or − will be calculated next.

For example,

A + B * C ↑ D

will be calculated as

(A) + (B * (C ↑ D))

such that first, C is raised to the D power, then this is multiplied by B, then this is added to A.

To avoid confusion, parentheses should be used. Then the rule is to calculate within a set of parentheses before moving on. Thus, the expression

(A + B) / (2 * C)

results in first determining the sum of A and B, then the product of 2 times C, and then the latter is divided into the former. Without the parentheses, the expression

A + B / 2 * C

results in B being divided by 2; then this is multiplied by C, and this is added to A.

You should also follow these rules:

1. Avoid dividing by zero.
   Some programs will have trouble if you attempt to divide by zero, such as 103/0, but in general you can expect an error message.
2. Balance your parentheses.
   This means you need to have the same number of parentheses on the left as on the right. If there is no match, you can expect an error message.

TRY IT

List the operations that the computer performs for the following statement:

    20   LET C = C/2 + 10

Suppose that before this statement, the value in space C is 88. What number will be in space C after this statement is executed? _____
The operations are as follows:

1. _____

2. _____

3. _____

4. _____

5. _____

Your answer should say that the value in C will be 54 after this statement is executed. The operations should include the following:

1. Find memory space C.
2. Take the number that is in memory space C (88).
3. Divide that number by 2 (88/2 = 44) and then add 10 (44 + 10 = 54).
4. Put that new number in space C, destroying whatever was there before.
5. Go on to the next statement.

TRY IT

Write a statement that will double the number that is in space F.

_____ LET _____

The Formula LET statement should be something like this:

```
20   LET F = 2 * F
```

Some common errors are to forget the multiplication sign, such as,

```
20  LET F = 2F
```

or to reverse the equals sign, such as,

```
20   LET 2 * F = F
```

TRY IT

Can you think of a way to determine what double the value of the number in space F is, and then to save in memory both the original and the new number? Write a statement that will double the number in F, and save both the old and new number.

_____   LET   _____

One possible answer is

```
20   LET F1 = 2 * F
```

Thus, space F will still contain the original value of F, and space F1 will contain the doubled value. Remember that only the address on the left of the equals sign is changed in a LET statement.

PROGRAM QUIZ

In this chapter you have learned how to increase the power of your programs by adding LET statements to those you already know— READ, DATA, PRINT, and END. To give you some practice in using LET statements in programs, the following problems are suggested.

(1) Suppose you find the following program. Tell what the output will be: _____
    Also, what goal does this program accomplish? _____

```
10    READ  X
20    DATA  7
30    LET  X  =  X ↑ 2
40    PRINT  X
50    END
```

The output will be 49 printed on the output screen. This program will take the number 7 and print out its square.

(2) Modify the following program so that it prints out both the number that is input and the square of the number.

```
10    READ  X
20    DATA  7
30    LET  X  =  X  ↑  2
40    PRINT  X
50    END
```

One way to accomplish this goal is to use two memory spaces:

```
10    READ  X
20    DATA  7
30    LET  Y  =  X ↑ 2
40    PRINT  X, Y
50    END
```

Note that line 30 could be written as

```
30    LET  Y  =  X * X
```

Another way (in some BASICs) is, simply, these four statements:

```
10    READ  X
20    DATA  7
30    PRINT  X,  X ↑ 2
40    END
```

This use of PRINT will be covered in chapter 9.

(3) Write a program to find the average score for John on his five quizzes. His scores were 50, 60, 70, 80, and 90.

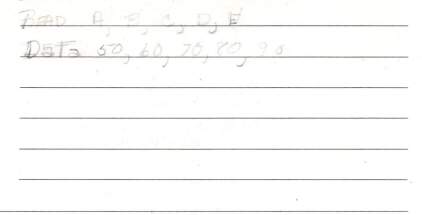

READ A, B, C, D, E

DATA 50, 60, 70, 80, 90

One way to accomplish this goal is the following program:

```
10   READ Q1, Q2, Q3, Q4, Q5
20   DATA 50, 60, 70, 80, 90
30   LET A = (Q1 + Q2 + Q3 + Q4 + Q5)/5
40   PRINT A
50   END
```

A shorter, but less general, way to do this is the following program:

```
10   LET A = (50 + 60 + 70 + 80 + 90)/5
20   PRINT A
30   END
```

As you can see, the first program can be easily modified for new data by using a different DATA statement; that makes it more general (and thus more desirable).

(4) Suppose that you have just written the following program to convert meters into inches. (Note that 1 meter equals approximately 39.4 inches.) Tell what the output will be: _____ What goal does this program accomplish? _____

```
10   LET I = 39.4 * M
20   LET M = 20
30   PRINT M, I
40   END
```

This program will print out two numbers: the first will be a 20, but we cannot be sure what the second will be. The goal of the program seems to have been to convert 20 meters to inches and then print out the value in both meters and inches. However, in line 10 the value of I is determined before we know what number is in space M.

(5) Alter the following program so that it will print out the value in meters and in inches.

```
10   LET I = 39.4 * M
20   LET M = 20
30   PRINT M, I
40   END
```

_____

_____

_____

_____

_____

_____

_____

One way to correct this program is as follows:

```
10   LET M = 20
20   LET I = 39.4 * M
30   PRINT M, I
40   END
```

Summary

In this chapter you have learned how to instruct the computer to perform computations with the LET statement. This new statement is crucial in solving the unit price problem. You should also try to see how this statement could be used, along with the READ, DATA, PRINT, and END statements, to solve other problems.

For example, if you wanted to build a computerized gradebook, the LET statement would be quite helpful in figuring out averages. Remember the example from Chapter 2 where our friend Sam had grades of 95, 85, and 75 on three exams. Based on what you have learned in this chapter, can you improve on the program that we wrote in the previous chapter?

```
10    READ E1, E2, E3
20    DATA 95, 85, 75
40    PRINT "FOR SAM"
60    PRINT "EXAM 1 SCORE IS" E1
70    PRINT "EXAM 2 SCORE IS" E2
80    PRINT "EXAM 3 SCORE IS" E3
99    END
```

Take a minute to work on this, and then go on below.

What is lacking here is a way to compute Sam's average score. To solve this problem, we must add a Formula LET statement and also a PRINT statement to tell us what the answer is.

```
10    READ E1, E2, E3
20    DATA 95, 85, 75
30    LET A = (E1 + E2 + E3)/3
40    PRINT "FOR SAM"
60    PRINT "EXAM 1 SCORE IS" E1
70    PRINT "EXAM 2 SCORE IS" E2
80    PRINT "EXAM 3 SCORE IS" E3
90    PRINT "AVERAGE SCORE IS" A
99    END
```

The above program will give an output that looks like this:

```
FOR SAM
EXAM 1 SCORE IS 95
EXAM 2 SCORE IS 85
EXAM 3 SCORE IS 75
AVERAGE SCORE IS 85
```

You might have also noticed another way you could have used LET statements in this problem. Instead of lines 10 and 20 you could have used Counter Set LET statements:

```
10    LET E1 = 95
15    LET E2 = 85
20    LET E3 = 75
```

What is wrong with this idea? It will give you the same answer as our other program, but it really customizes the program too specifically for Sam. If we have many other students, it is better to use a more general form of the program; in this way, each new person just needs a new DATA card (also the PRINT statement at line 40 will need to be changed for persons other than Sam).

Can you think of a way that an Arithmetic LET statement might have been used? We could erase lines 10, 20, and 30, and replace them with the following:

```
30   LET A = (95 + 85 + 75)/3
```

What would happen to our program then? Would we get the correct average printed out? Yes, we would, since line 30 computes the average and line 90 prints it out. However, the computer would be at a loss when it came to lines 60, 70, and 80 since nothing was ever put into these memory spaces. Also, the program would not be as general as our original one. Thus in the present case, the Formula LET statement at line 30 seems to be best for the job!

4

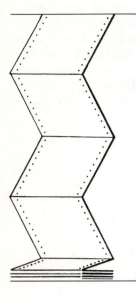

Introduction to Transfer of Control

Overview

So far we have modified our pocket calculator by adding many more memory spaces—and so we needed READ and DATA statements to get information into them and PRINT statements to get it out. Then we modified it by simplifying the instructions for computations—as in the three kinds of LET statements. What further improvements can we make?

Remember that when you operate a calculator, you are in charge of the order in which steps are carried out—you are the executive control component of the system because you must instruct the calculator about each step one at a time. In computer systems, however, the CPU will take over this job. Normally, a program will be executed in order, starting with the first line and working down. However, there are many cases in which you may want to change the order. In this chapter you will learn about two statements (GO TO and IF) that allow you to transfer control from one part of the program to another. This transfer-of-control feature gives you more power in instructing the computer.

For example, consider the unit price problem. Let's say that you are looking for peanut butter that costs less than 10¢ per ounce so you want the program to call your attention to any brand that meets your test. Thus, the program in the Overview of chapter 3 could be modified by adding lines 90 and 95:

```
10   READ T, N
20   DATA 103, 12
30   LET U = T/N
40   PRINT "TOTAL COST IS" T
60   PRINT "NUMBER OF OUNCES IS" N
80   PRINT "UNIT COST IS" U
90   IF U >= 10 THEN 99
95   PRINT "THATS CHEAP"
99   END
```

In this case, line 90 tells the computer to go to line 99 if the value of U is greater than or equal to 10 but to go to line 95 otherwise. Thus the computer will print out THATS CHEAP only if the unit price is less than a dime. If you were to perform this job on your calculator, you would have to make the decision at line 90, but when you are using BASIC you can instruct the computer to make the decision for you!

What Is Transfer of Control?

Remember that a program is just a list of statements. Normally, the computer will execute each statement in order, beginning with the one at the top of the list, then going on to the one directly below it, and so on down the list. You can think of this in the following way: the program list is inserted into the computer, then the pointer arrow will point to the first statement; when this statement is executed it will point to the next statement, and so on.

However, it is possible to tell the computer to go from some line in the program to some other line in the program that is not directly below it. For example, consider what happens if line 90 in the unit price example is

    90   GO TO 99

unconditional branch

This moves the pointer arrow from line 90 to line 99, thus ignoring line 95. Thus the GO TO statement can be used to make an **unconditional branch** in a program. An unconditional branch is a type of transfer of control in which the pointer arrow moves from one line of the program to another line of the program that is not necessarily the next line.

It is also possible to tell the computer to jump to some other line in the program under certain conditions. For example, line 90 in the unit price example was

    90   IF U >= 10 THEN 99

conditional branch

This would move the pointer arrow from line 90 to line 99 only if the value in memory space U was equal to or greater than 10; otherwise the pointer arrow would move on to the next line (95). Thus, the IF statement allows you to make a **conditional branch.** A conditional branch is a type of transfer of control in which the pointer arrow follows one path under one condition and follows another path under another condition.

Thus the GO TO and IF statements allow you to transfer control (that is, move the pointer arrow) to a specific line in the program. This chapter will focus on how to make conditional and unconditional branches in a program. In particular this chapter will focus on

branching programs

branching programs—programs that have two alternative routes, with both routes starting at the same line and coming together again at the same line. As an example of a familiar branching program, consider the following recipe:

1. Take a bowl.
2. Put in 2 cups of flour.
3. If you are on a diet go to line 8, otherwise go on.
4. Put in ½ cup of cream.
5. Put in ½ cup butter.

6. Put in 3 eggs.
7. Go to step 11.
8. Put in ½ cup skimmed milk.
9. Put in ½ cup margarine.
10. Put in 3 egg substitutes.
11. Mix for 3 minutes.
12. Pour into a baking pan.
13. Put pan into oven for 20 minutes at 400 degrees.
14. Take out pan, and let cool.
15. That's all.

Notice that step 3 involves a conditional branch; you must decide whether or not you want to follow a diet recipe or a non-diet recipe. For a diet recipe the steps are 1, 2, 3, 8, 9, 10, 11, 12, 13, 14, 15. For a non-diet recipe the steps are 1, 2, 3, 4, 5, 6, 7, 11, 12, 13, 14, 15. Notice that step 7 involves an unconditional branch. This allows both branches of the program to return to the same place in the program—both the diet and non-diet branches rejoin at line 11.

In this chapter you will learn how to tell the computer to jump to a particular line in the program. Remember that each line in a program has a unique line number, and that the computer organizes the statements into a program list beginning with the lowest line number and going to the highest. Even if you have the line numbers out of order, the computer will execute them in order. Normally, the computer will execute statements in the following order: first, all DATA statements will be executed (in order of their line numbers if there is more than one), then the pointer arrow will point to the lowest line number at the top of the program. When that statement is executed the arrow will move down one line to the next highest line number, when that statement is executed the arrow will move one line down, and so on. Each time the computer finishes a statement it will then move on to one immediately below it, that is, the one with the next highest line number. Thus, with the statements you have learned so far you can write sequential programs—programs where the computer starts at the top and the arrow moves down one statement at a time. However, by using two additional statements—GO TO and IF—it is possible to tell the computer to jump (i.e., move the pointer arrow) to some other statement, out of sequence, or to jump under certain circumstances.

GO TO Statements

The first kind of transfer-of-control statement you will learn tells the computer to move its pointer arrow to a particular line number. The format of this statement is

line
number   GO TO   line
                           number

where a line number goes in the blank on the left of GO TO and a line number goes in the blank on the right of GO TO. Remember that each statement of a program has its own line and each line has its own unique line number.

For example, the statement

    100   GO TO 150

means that the computer is in the following state just before this statement is executed:

▶ *The computer has just finished the statement just above GO TO 150 on the program.*

(Or the computer may just have finished a statement that transferred control to line 100, such as:

    55   GO TO 100.)

After this statement is executed the computer will be in the following state:

▶ *The computer will be working on the statement on line 150, having skipped any statements between line 100 and line 150.*

The operations performed for the statement

    100   GO TO 150

are as follows:

1. Take the pointer arrow from line 100 and move it to line 150.
2. Do not execute any statements between lines 100 and 150.
3. After executing the statement on line 150, move the arrow to the line immediately below 150 (unless 150 is another GO TO or IF statement).

TRY IT

Suppose that two lines of your program are as follows:

    30   GO TO 50
    50   GO TO 30

How many loops would occur? _____
Describe the course of the pointer arrow when it reaches line 30.

This part of the program would create a vicious loop. The pointer arrow would go from line 30 to line 50 to line 30 to line 50 and so on until interrupted by the computer center operator or by depressing the break key at the terminal or by shutting the power off. Otherwise this silly jumping back and forth could go on forever.

TRY IT

Write a statement that will cause the computer to move from line 10 to line 100 of the program.

——————   GO TO   ——————————————————

A statement that will accomplish this goal is the following:

    10   GO TO 100

Of course, the assumption is that there are statements between 10 and 100. Otherwise

    10 —————
    100 —————

does the trick, too.

IF Statements

Another statement that controls the order in which statements are performed is the **IF statement.** The IF statement allows you to tell the computer to move to a particular line number only if some simple condition is met, and otherwise to go on with the next statement in the program. The format of the IF statement is

line number	IF	number or address name	relation	number or address name		line number
—————	IF (	—————	—————	—————)	THEN	—————

relational symbol   where a line number goes in the first blank, an address name goes in the first blank to the right of IF, a **relational symbol** goes in the next blank (such as *less than, less than or equal to, equal to, greater than,* *greater than or equal to, not equal to,* or *approximately equal*), a number or address name goes in the third blank after IF, and a line number goes after THEN. The symbols for the seven relationships are listed in the following Style Box.

STYLE BOX: Relational Symbols

IF statements can use seven types of relational symbols:

$<$	means *less than*
$<=$	means *less than or equal to*
$=$	means *equal to*
$>$	means *greater than*
$>=$	means *greater than or equal to*
$<>$	means *not equal to*
$==$	means *approximately equal*

For example, the statement

```
90   IF U >= 10 THEN 99
```

means that the computer is in the following state before this statement is executed:

▶ *There is a number stored in memory space U and the statement just before this one in the program has been completed.*

After this statement has been executed, the computer will be in the following state:

▶ *If the number stored in memory space U is 10 or more, then the computer will be working on the statement at line 99, or if the number in space U is less than 10, the computer will be working on the statement just below this IF statement.*

The operations performed for the statement

```
90   IF U >= 10 THEN 99
```

are as follows:

1. Find memory space U.
2. Compare the number in space U with 10.
3. If the number in space U is not 10 or more, just move the pointer arrow to the statement immediately after line 90 on the program and continue normally.
4. If the number in memory space U is 10 or more, move the pointer arrow to line 99, start working on the statement at line

99, ignore all lines between 90 and 99, and work normally down from line 99.

TRY IT

List the operations that the computer will perform for the following statement:

    50   IF X2 = X3 THEN 100

The steps are as follows:

1. _____

2. _____

3. _____

4. _____

The steps would be the following:

1. Find memory spaces X2 and X3 but do not destroy the numbers in them.
2. Compare the number in X2 with the number in X3.
3. If they do not match, go on to the next step after line 50.
4. If they do match, move the pointer arrow directly to line 100, and continue down from there.

TRY IT

Write a statement to move the pointer to line 500 only if the number in memory space C is 0. Assume the computer is on line 10.

_____   IF   _____

The following statement would accomplish this goal:

    10   IF C = 0 THEN 500

PROGRAM QUIZ

Until this chapter you have been able to write only sequential programs, that is, programs that start at the top and move straight down to the bottom of the list. Now you have added two statements to your repertoire that allow you to create transfers of control. In the next chapter you will learn more about the nature of these transfers, but this Program Quiz will focus on some simple applications of the IF and GO TO statements. In particular, this program quiz will focus on simple branching programs—programs that have two alternative routes that come together at the same line of a program.

(1) Suppose you have the following sequential program:

```
20  PRINT "THIS IS FUN"
30  END
```

Modify this program so that the message will be printed out repeatedly.

_____

_____

_____

_____

_____

The way to accomplish this goal is to build in a loop such as the following:

```
20  PRINT "THIS IS FUN"
25  GO TO 20
30  END
```

Note that this program creates a potentially infinite loop. The computer will never get to line 30. Instead the computer will continue to print out the message until it is stopped by some external operating command. (See the Appendix for how to stop a running program.)

(2) Suppose that you answered the previous question by generating this program:

```
10  GO TO 20
20  PRINT "THIS IS FUN"
30  END
```

How many times would the message be printed out? _____

_____

In this case the message would be printed out only one time since the sequence of statements is as follows: begin at line 10, then go to line 20 and print out the message, then go to line 30 and stop. In this case line 10 is not needed, and the output would be the same without it.

(3) Suppose you have the following sequential program:

```
20   PRINT "THIS IS FUN"
30   END
```

You want to modify it so that it will print "THIS IS FUN" if the number in memory space A is equal to 2 and it will print "THIS IS NOT FUN" if the number in space A is not equal to 2. Write a program to accomplish this goal.

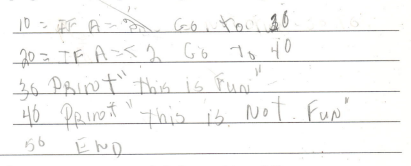

```
10 = IF A = 2, Go too 30
20 = IF A =< 2 Go To 40
30 PRint "this is Fun"
40 PRint "this is Not Fun"
50 END
```

A preferred way to accomplish this goal is as follows:

```
10   IF A = 2 THEN 50
20   PRINT "THIS IS NOT FUN"
30   GO TO 60
50   PRINT "THIS IS FUN"
60   END
```

Note that the pointer arrow will start at line 10, but it will jump to line 50 if the number in space A is equal to 2. The most common error is to leave out line 30. Consider what would happen without the GO TO statement. For cases when the number in A is 2, everything will work fine; the "THIS IS FUN" message will be printed out. However, if the number in space A is not 2, the computer will print out two messages: "THIS IS NOT FUN" and "THIS IS FUN." You might have thought that you should put an END statement after the first PRINT statement; for example, you could erase line 30 and replace it with the following:

```
30   END
```

Can you see that this would give you the desired results? Even though this might give you the desired results, it is not good programming practice to have more than one END statement. It is good to develop healthy programming habits early because when you start writing more complex programs, having several END statements could lead to problems.

(4) Suppose you are given the following program:

```
10   IF X = Y THEN 40
20   PRINT "YOU ARE WRONG"
30   GO TO 50
40   PRINT "YOU ARE RIGHT"
50   END
```

What is accomplished by this program? _____
What steps are performed for the statement on line 10?

1. _____

2. _____

3. _____

4. _____

The problem solved by this program is: "Print out 'YOU ARE WRONG' if the number in memory space X is not equal to the number in memory space Y, and print out 'YOU ARE RIGHT' if they are equal." The steps involved in line 10 are as follows:

1. Check the numbers in memory spaces X and Y.
2. Determine whether or not they match.
3. If they do match, shift the pointer arrow to line 40 and continue on down from there.
4. If not, shift the pointer arrow to the next line (line 20) and go on down from there.

Summary

You have learned the basics about two statements that allow you to specify the order in which statements are executed. In the next two chapters you will learn more about how useful these statements can be. However, for now, it is important that you see how transfer of control can improve your programs. For example, in the unit price problem, you can now have the computer categorize peanut butter products into acceptable and unacceptable buys.

How would you apply this newly found feature to improving our gradebook problem (discussed in the Summary of Chapter 3)? Remember that Sam scored 95 on exam 1, 85 on exam 2, and 75 on exam 3, and that we wanted to keep a computerized gradebook. Could we use the transfer-of-control statements (IF and GO TO) to let our program assign grades? Let's say that an average of 90 to 100 is A, 80 to below 90 is B, 70 to below 80 is C, and below 70 is not passing. How would you modify the following program?

```
10    READ E1, E2, E3
20    DATA 95, 85, 75
30    LET A = (E1 + E2 + E3)/3
40    PRINT "FOR SAM"
60    PRINT "EXAM 1 SCORE IS" E1
70    PRINT "EXAM 2 SCORE IS" E2
80    PRINT "EXAM 3 SCORE IS" E3
90    PRINT "AVERAGE SCORE IS" A
99    END
```

Take all the time you need and try to improve this program.

We need a system for assigning grades based on the person's average score. For example, we could erase line 99 and add the following lines to solve this problem:

```
100   IF A >= 70 THEN 120
110   PRINT "NOT PASSING"
115   GO TO 999
120   IF A >= 80 THEN 140
130   PRINT "GRADE IS C"
135   GO TO 999
140   IF A >= 90 THEN 160
150   PRINT "GRADE IS B"
155   GO TO 999
160   PRINT "GRADE IS A"
999   END
```

To test what we have written, let's see what happens if the average is 65. At line 100 it fails the test, so the next step is 110 ("NOT PASS-ING" is printed), then the next step is 115 and this transfers control to 999 and the program ends. For an average grade of 95, the pointer arrow would move from line 100 to line 120, then to line 140, then to line 160, and finally to 999. In the case of our friend Sam, the print-out will be as follows:

```
FOR  SAM
EXAM  1  SCORE  IS    95
EXAM  2  SCORE  IS    85
EXAM  3  SCORE  IS    75
AVERAGE  SCORE  IS  85
GRADE  IS  B
```

One of the major mistakes that people make is to leave off the GO TO statements at lines 115, 135, and 145. Trace the results of this mistake for a score of 65. Can you see that too much would be printed out?

5

Types of Transfer of Control

Overview

Much power is added to our computer system, as compared to our simple pocket calculator, when the computer can make choices and perform repetitive operations. In the previous chapter we emphasized the ability to make choices. For example, in the unit price problem, the computer prints out "THATS CHEAP" under some circumstances but not under others. This is called **branching** *because the computer makes a decision and then follows one program branch or another based on its decision.*

branching

In this chapter we will emphasize the ability to perform repetitive operations.

In the unit price problem, if you used a calculator you would have to enter the numbers and operations for each product you were interested in. In this chapter you will learn how to use IF and GO TO statements to form loops; thus you will be able to find out many unit prices using the same program. As you will see, looping, or re-using a section of a program, can save you a lot of time and energy—especially as compared to using a calculator.

Let's look at the unit price problem again, with new IF and GO TO statements included. Suppose we had a 12-ounce jar at $1.03, a 7-ounce jar at 66¢, and a 9.5 ounce jar at 79¢. We want to use the same program to solve each problem. Our program could be the following:

```
10   READ T, N
20   DATA 103, 12, 66, 7, 79, 9.5
30   LET U = T/N
40   PRINT "TOTAL COST IS" T
60   PRINT "NUMBER OF OUNCES IS" N
80   PRINT "UNIT COST IS" U
90   IF U >= 10 THEN 10
95   PRINT "THATS CHEAP"
97   GO TO 10
99   END
```

This program adds one new line (line 97) and modifies one line (90) for the program given in the Overview of chapter 4. This program will put 103 in memory space T, 12 in space N, compute the value of U, print out the three values, and then recycle to line 10. This time it will put 66 into space T, 7 into space N, and so on. On the fourth branch back up to line 10, the computer will find that it is out of data when it tries to read into space T and this will cause the computer to end the program. On the screen will appear the following:

```
TOTAL COST IS 103
NUMBER OF OUNCES IS 12
UNIT COST IS 8.583333
THATS CHEAP
TOTAL COST IS 66
NUMBER OF OUNCES IS 7
UNIT COST IS 9.4285714
THATS CHEAP
TOTAL COST IS 79
NUMBER OF OUNCES IS 9.5
UNIT COST IS 8.3157894
THATS CHEAP
OUT OF DATA AT LINE 10
```

Then the program will end. (The OUT OF DATA message may vary with different versions of BASIC.) After reading this chapter, you will be able to re-use programs, that is, you will be able to form loops.

Looping and Nonlooping Programs

In the previous chapter you learned about transferring control by using the GO TO and IF statements. There are many ways to use these statements, and one major distinction is between **looping** and *nonlooping* programs. In the previous chapter we emphasized **nonlooping jumps**—a transfer that avoided any possible repetition of statements such as a jump from one line of the program to a line further down the program. For example, the unit price program in chapter 4 contained the following statement:

looping

nonlooping jumps

```
90   IF U >= 10 THEN 99
```

In this case control is transferred from line 90 to a line below it (99) if the condition is met and to another line below it (95 PRINT "THATS CHEAP") if not. This is a nonlooping jump because no statement in the program is executed more than once.

In this chapter we added a new line to the unit price program:

```
97   GO TO 10
```

We also modified one line:

```
90   IF U >= 10 THEN 10
```

This turns our unit price program into a looping program because lines 10 through 97 can be repeated over and over. Thus in looping programs the GO TO and/or IF statements are used to allow repetition, but in a nonlooping program the GO TO and IF statements do not result in repetition.

As another example of the difference between a looping and a nonlooping program, consider the recipe discussed in the previous chapter. The left side of Figure 8 gives a pictorial representation of the two paths; they both start at the top and end at the bottom with no step executed more than once. Now consider the following recipe:

1. Take a bowl.
2. Put in 2 cups of flour.
3. Put in ½ cup of cream.
4. Put in ½ cup of butter.
5. Put in 3 eggs.
6. If you need more batter for the pan, go back to step 2; otherwise go on.
7. Mix for 3 minutes.
8. Pour into baking pan.
9. Put pan into oven for 20 minutes at 400 degrees.
10. Take out pan, and let cool.
11. That's all.

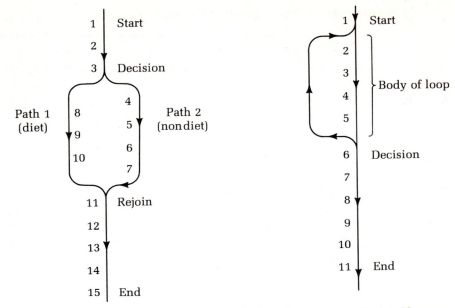

A *(Nonlooping) Branching Program.* No
steps are repeated.

A *Looping Program.* Body of loop can be
repeated.

Figure 8.   *Recipe with Loop.*

Notice that step 6 involves a decision: you must decide whether
you need more batter. If so, you repeat steps 2, 3, 4, and 5; if not, you
go on to step 8 and so on. This allows for looping since steps 2, 3, 4,
and 5 can be repeated. The right side of Figure 8 shows a looping
program.

Chapter 4 emphasized only nonlooping uses of IF and GO TO,
such as cases in which the pointer arrow moved from one line to a line
further down in the program. This chapter will emphasize looping
uses of IF and GO TO, such as cases when the pointer arrow is moved
from one line of the program to a line that comes above. To better
understand how IF and GO TO can be used to form both looping and
nonlooping jumps, let's consider four common situations. These
four are not the only ways to use transfer-of-control statements;
however, they are useful in many cases. The four situations are
as follows:

Repeating a READ-in. This is a looping situation in which the
pointer arrow moves from a lower line in the program back up

to a READ statement. Thus the next numbers waiting at the input window are read in, as occurs in the jump from line 97 to line 10 in our revised unit price program.

Branching Down. This is a nonlooping situation in which the pointer arrow goes to one part of the program under one condition and to another part under other conditions. The unit price and gradebook programs in Chapter 4 are examples.

Waiting for a Specific Data Number. This is a looping situation that continues until a specific number is read into the computer.

Waiting for a Counter to Reach a Certain Number. This is a looping situation that continues until a counter reaches a certain number.

For each type of looping situation you must be careful to remember to consider each of the following conditions:

initial condition   **Initial Condition.** What is the state of the computer at the beginning of the first loop?

exit condition   **Exit Condition.** What conditions must exist for the pointer arrow to shift outside of the loop?

body of the loop   **Body of the Loop.** What operations are performed each time the loop is executed?

reset condition   **Reset Condition.** How is the program reset back to the start of the loop?

Repeating a READ-in

Suppose that you have a program that reads in two numbers (such as total cost and number of ounces), then performs some calculation on these numbers (such as determining the unit price), prints the result, and then ends. This is a nonlooping program because each statement is executed only one time. As an example, consider the following nonlooping program:

```
10   READ T, N
20   DATA 103, 12
30   LET U = T/N
40   PRINT U
99   END
```

The program will put number 103 in space T, 12 in space N, compute the value of U and put the result in U, then print out the result.

Suppose that we have a list of data at the input window, such as the cost and ounces for several products. How can we instruct the computer to print unit prices for each? One way to accomplish this is as follows:

```
10    READ T, N
20    DATA 103, 12
30    LET U = T/N
40    PRINT U
50    READ T, N
60    DATA 66, 7
70    LET U = T/N
80    PRINT U
90    READ T, N
100   DATA 79, 9.5
110   LET U = T/N
120   PRINT U
130   END
```

In this case, three unit prices would be computed and printed out. However, as you can see, each time a new unit price is determined, many more lines must be added to the program.

To have the computer repeat the process without having to add many new lines to your program, you can use a repeating-a-READ-in format, such as the following:

```
10    READ T, N
20    DATA 103, 12, 66, 7, 79, 9.5
30    LET U = T/N
40    PRINT U
50    GO TO 10
99    END
```

The program will read 103 into space T and 12 into N, make a computation, print the result, and then recycle back to the READ statement. Here it will read in the next two numbers, calculate, print, and recycle back to READ again, and so on. When the computer loops to the READ statement for the fourth time, the computer will try to read the next number but there is none, so it has found the exit condition. The computer will stop and print "OUT OF DATA." In this case the initial condition is that a list of numbers is waiting at the input window and the first two are read into memory; the body of the loop executes a calculation and prints out a number; the reset instruction is to loop back from line 50 to line 10; and the exit condition is to stop and print "OUT OF DATA" when there are no more numbers waiting at the input window.

The general format for the **repeating a READ-in loop** is:

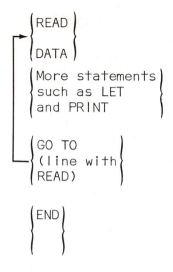

The *initial condition* is that numbers are waiting at the input window, and one or more are read in.

The *body of the loop* consists of a series of statements such as LET and PRINT that operate on the numbers that are read in.

The *reset* statement sends the pointer arrow back to the original state so that the next numbers will be processed in the same loop as was just executed.

The *exit* condition is that there are no more numbers at the window. If the computer tries to execute a READ but there are no numbers left, it will end the program and print "OUT OF DATA."

As an example, consider a program to read in a number and print it, such as the following:

```
10   READ X
20   DATA 6, 8, 19, 20
30   PRINT X
40   END
```

This program will put the number 6 in memory space X, then print out the number in X (which is 6), and then will stop. The output will be the number 6.

To have the computer repeat this process, you must use the repeating-a-READ-in format:

```
10   READ X
20   DATA 6, 8, 19, 20
30   PRINT X
40   GO TO 10
50   END
```

This program will read a 6 into memory space X, then print the 6, then it will loop back to the initial state and read an 8 into space X, then print the 8, then it will loop back again, and read in 19 and print 19, then it will loop back and read 20 into space X, and then print 20. When it loops for the fifth time, the computer will try to read the next number but there is none, so it has found the exit condition. The computer will stop and print "OUT OF DATA." In this case, the initial condition is that a series of numbers is waiting (6, 8, 19, and

20) and the first one is read into memory; the body of the loop is to print out the number, the reset instruction is to loop back to line 10, and the exit condition is to stop and write "OUT OF DATA" when there are no more numbers waiting at the input window.

STYLE BOX: How is READ like IF?

The READ statement is like an IF statement because it always involves an exit test. If there is a number waiting in line at the input window, then the number is inserted into the appropriate memory space as indicated in the READ statement. However, if there are no more numbers at the input window, then the exit condition has been reached: the computer will print "OUT OF DATA" on the output screen and then stop working on the program (as if it came to an END statement).

The rule is this:

▶ *If there is no more data and the computer comes to a READ statement, it will print "OUT OF DATA" and stop.*

TRY IT

Suppose you have written a program to convert feet into meters, such as the following:

```
10   READ F
20   DATA 1, 2, 3, 4
30   LET M = .31 * F
40   PRINT F, M
50   GO TO 10
60   END
```

What will be the output of this program?

_____

_____

_____

_____

_____

The output will look like this:

```
1    .31000
2    .62000
3    .93000
4   1.24000
OUT OF DATA AT LINE 10
```

Briefly, the computer will perform the following operations: put 1 into memory space F, destroying whatever was there previously; multiply 1 times .31 and put the answer in space M destroying whatever was there before; then print out 1 and .31000 (M); then repeat these steps for 2, 3, and 4. Note that the computer never gets to line 60.

TRY IT

Suppose you have written a sequential program for printing out a temperature in Celsius given a number measured on the Fahrenheit scale.

```
10   READ F
15   DATA 32
20   LET C = (F−32)*(5/9)
30   PRINT F, C
40   END
```

The output of this program will be as follows:

```
32          0
```

Modify this program so that you could print out the Celsius values for each of the following Fahrenheit temperatures: 32, 0, 100, 72.

_____

_____

_____

_____

_____

_____

Your new program just needs a repeating-a-READ-in, such as:

```
10   READ F
15   DATA 32
16   DATA 0, 100, 72
20   LET C = (F-32)*(5/9)
30   PRINT F, C
35   GO TO 10
40   END
```

The output of this program would be the following:

```
32     0
0      -17.7777777
100    37.7777777
72     22.2222222
OUT OF DATA AT LINE 10
```

You could have put all the data on one DATA card (or on one line—15) and obtained the same results.

Branching Down

Suppose you read in numbers from the line waiting at the input window, you perform some operations on them if certain conditions are met but you perform other operations if other conditions are met, and then you exit to the same line. This situation has two possible branches; they contain different instructions but they both end at the same place.

For example, consider these two programs. For the one on the left you compute the unit price per ounce, but for the one on the right you compute the unit price per pound.

```
10   READ T, N                      10   READ T, N
20   DATA 103, 12, 66, 7, 79, 9.5   20   DATA 103, 12, 66, 7, 79, 9.5
30   LET U = T/N                    30   LET U = T/(N/16)
40   PRINT "PER OUNCE" U            40   PRINT "PER POUND" U
50   GO TO 10                       50   GO TO 10
99   END                           99   END
```

Suppose you wanted to use the program on the left when the number of ounces (N) is less than 16 (i.e., less than 1 pound) and the one on the right otherwise. You could sort your data by hand and decide which program to use (as you would with a calculator), or you could use a branch in your computer program. Note that both programs are looping programs (i.e., repeating READ-in loop), so we will branch to one of two looping programs.

These two programs can be combined into a single program that branches one way for values of N less than 16 and another way for all other values of N.

```
10    READ T, N
20    DATA 103, 12, 66, 7, 79, 9.5
30    IF N >= 16 THEN 70
40    LET U = T/N
50    PRINT "PER OUNCE" U
60    GO TO 10
70    LET U = T/(N/16)
80    PRINT "PER POUND" U
90    GO TO 10
99    END
```

This program will put 103 into space T, then 12 into N, and then will see if it should jump to branch 2 (at line 70). If not, it will calculate a value for U at line 40, then print it at line 50, and then return from line 60 to line 10. If the value of N is 16 or more, the pointer arrow moves from line 30 to line 70, then line 80, then line 90 and back up to 10. In the above situation three unit prices will be printed out (all based on the first branch) and then the computer will print "OUT OF DATA."

The initial condition is that numbers are read in from the line waiting at the window. In this case, the exit condition is better called a decision condition since here a decision is made concerning which path to take. The decision condition is whether the number is less than 16 or not; if so, the pointer arrow jumps to branch 2 (at lines 70 to 90) and if not, it stays on branch 1 (lines 40 to 60). The body of the loop is to LET and PRINT in branch 1 or to LET and PRINT in branch 2. The reset instruction is the GO TO statement (at lines 60 and 90) that allows both branches to return to the same place in the program (line 10).

The format of a **branching** program is as follows:

$\begin{Bmatrix} \text{READ} \\ \text{DATA} \end{Bmatrix}$ The initial condition is that numbers are waiting at the input window and one or more are read in.

$\begin{Bmatrix} \text{IF} \\ \end{Bmatrix}$ The decision (exit) condition is whether the number that is read in meets some value. If so, then the pointer arrow shifts to branch 2; if not it goes on to branch 1.

$\begin{Bmatrix} \text{Statements for} \\ \text{branch 1} \end{Bmatrix}$ The body of the loop has two parts: the body of the loop for branch 1 and the body of the loop for branch 2.

$\left.\begin{array}{l}\text{GO TO}\\\text{line with}\\\text{READ}\end{array}\right\}$　　　The reset sends the pointer arrow back to the same point in the program for both branches.

$\left.\begin{array}{l}\text{Statements for}\\\text{branch 2}\end{array}\right\}$　　　The body of the loop for branch 2.

$\left.\begin{array}{l}\text{GO TO}\\\text{(line with}\\\text{READ)}\end{array}\right\}$　　　The reset for branch 2.

```
END
```

TRY IT

Here is a program involving Celsius scale numbers. What does this program do?

```
10   READ C
20   DATA 0, 10, 20, 30
30   IF C >= 22.22 THEN 50
40   PRINT "ITS COLD", C
45   GO TO 10
50   PRINT "ITS HOT", C
60   GO TO 10
70   END
```

What is the output of this program?

_____

_____

_____

_____

_____

This is a sorting program. If a number is greater than 22.22 Centigrade (i.e., 72 Fahrenheit), the computer prints out "ITS HOT" along with the temperature. If the number is less than or equal to 22.22, then the computer prints out "ITS COLD" with the number. The output will be as follows.

```
ITS  COLD   0
ITS  COLD   10
ITS  COLD   20
ITS  HOT    30
OUT OF DATA AT LINE 10
```

TRY IT

Suppose you wanted to sort Celsius temperatures into pleasant and unpleasant temperatures. Let's say the pleasant range is between 15 to 25. Write a program that will take these numbers as data: 0, 10, 20, 30; and then will print out "ITS NICE" with the number if it falls in the pleasant range but will print out "STAY HOME" with the number if it does not.

One solution is as follows:

```
10    READ T
20    DATA 0, 10, 20, 30
30    IF T < 15 THEN 60
40    IF T > 25 THEN 60
50    PRINT "ITS NICE", T
55    GO TO 10
60    PRINT "STAY HOME", T
65    GO TO 10
70    END
```

Notice that in this program there are two IF statements. They allow you to branch down to the "unpleasant" branch if either of the conditions (below 15 or above 25) is met.

Waiting for a Data Number

Suppose that you would like to use the repeating READ-in loop but you want to avoid the OUT OF DATA message. For example, in a longer program you may want the computer to go on to another part of the program once it is finished reading in and operating on the data. You could add an exit condition so that the program will shift down to a lower line number if a certain data number is read in. Then you could insert that number as the last one in line (i.e., the last number in the last DATA statement).

For example, we could start with a program like this:

```
10   READ T, N
20   DATA 103, 12, 66, 7, 79, 9.5
30   LET U = T/N
40   PRINT U
50   GO TO 10
99   END
```

Then to avoid the OUT OF DATA message that would occur, we could add a new exit condition such as in line 25.

```
10   READ T, N
20   DATA 103, 12, 66, 7, 79, 9.5, .999
25   IF T = .999 THEN 99
30   LET U = T/N
40   PRINT U
50   GO TO 10
99   END
```

The initial condition is that seven numbers are waiting at the input window, with the first pair being read into memory. The exit condition is that the number in space T is .999; if it is, then the pointer arrow will exit from the loop and jump to line 99. The body of the loop is just to print out the number. The reset statement is to go back to line 10.

Thus the format for the **waiting-for-a-Data number loop** is as follows:

$\left\{\begin{array}{l}\text{READ}\\\text{DATA}\end{array}\right\}$	The initial condition is that numbers are waiting at the input window, and one is read in.
$\left\{\begin{array}{l}\text{IF (exit line}\\\text{with END)}\end{array}\right\}$	The exit condition is that if a certain number is read in from the line at the input window, then the pointer arrow will shift to a lower line such as the END line.
More statements	The body of the loop consists of the series of statements after the exit decision but before the reset statement.
GO TO (line with READ)	The reset statement puts the pointer arrow back at the READ statement and allows for another cycle through the loop.
END	

TRY IT

Suppose you have written a program with a repeating-a-READ-in loop such as the following:

```
10    READ F
20    DATA 1, 2, 3, 4
30    LET M = .31 * F
40    PRINT F, M
50    GO TO 10
60    END
```

Modify this program so that it will avoid the OUT OF DATA message.

One way to accomplish this goal is to use a waiting-for-a-Data-number loop such as the following:

```
10    READ F
20    DATA 1, 2, 3, 4, .9999
30    IF F = .9999 THEN 90
40    LET M = .31 * F
50    PRINT F, M
60    GO TO 10
90    END
```

In this case the order of line execution is: 10, 20, 30, 40, 50, 60, 10, 20, 30, 40, 50, 60, 10, 20, 30, 40, 50, 60, 10, 20, 30, 40, 50, 60, 10, 20, 30, 90.

TRY IT

In the previous example, suppose the IF statement came instead at line 55. How would that influence the output? _____

Now suppose that the IF statement came at line 65. How would that influence the output? _____

_____

_____

Remember that the original program is as follows:

```
10   READ F
20   DATA 1, 2, 3, 4, .9999
30   IF F = .9999 THEN 90
40   LET M = .31 * F
50   PRINT F, M
60   GO TO 10
90   END
```

If the IF were moved to line 55 the output would include .9999 in it but there would be no OUT OF DATA message:

```
1          .31
2          .62
3          .93
4         1.24
.9999     .309979
```

If the IF were moved to line 65 it would never be executed. Each time the pointer arrow came to line 60 it would return to line 10. Thus the output would be as follows:

```
1          .31
2          .62
3          .93
4         1.24
.9999     .309979
OUT OF DATA
```

Waiting for a Counter

The last way to use the IF and GO TO statements that we will look at in this chapter is to wait for a counter to reach a certain value. Each time the pointer arrow moves through the body of the loop, a counter is incremented (e.g., a number is added to it). When the counter reaches a certain value, the pointer arrow shifts outside the loop to a lower part of the program.

As an example, consider the following program:

```
10   READ T, N
20   DATA 103, 12, 66, 7, 79, 9.5
30   LET U = T/N
40   PRINT U
50   GO TO 10
99   END
```

This program will compute and print out three numbers and then print "OUT OF DATA" on the fourth loop back to line 10.

To convert this program into a waiting-for-a-counter loop, we must first set a counter to zero (at line 5), then allow it to be incremented by 1 each time the pointer arrow moves through the body of the loop (at line 45), and we must maintain the reset condition at line 50. The revised version is as follows:

```
 5   LET C = 0
10   READ T, N
20   DATA 103, 12, 66, 7, 79, 9.5
30   LET U = T/N
40   PRINT U
45   LET C = C + 1
50   IF C < 3 THEN 10
99   END
```

In this case, the computer will set memory space C to zero, then put 103 in T and 12 in N, compute a value for U, print the value, change the number in C to 1, decide to jump back up to line 10. On this second recycle, 66 is put into T, 7 into N, the value is computed and printed, and C is incremented to 2. Since C is still less than 3 the pointer arrow moves up to line 10 for the third cycle. In this cycle 79 is read into T, 9.5 into N, a value is computed and printed, C is incremented to 3, and now the exit condition is met when a test is made at line 50 (because now C is equal to 3). The pointer arrow moves down to the next line (99) and the program ends.

The initial condition is that the counter is zero. The exit condition is that the counter is not less than 3. The body of the loop is to read, compute, and print a number. The reset statement is to increment the counter and then go to line 10.

The format for a **waiting-for-a-Counter loop** is as follows:

```
(part of program)
LET C = 0
```
The initial condition is that the counter is set to zero (or some other value).

```
(body of loop)
LET C = C + 1
```
The body of the loop may contain statements such as LET and PRINT and the like.

```
IF C < 3 THEN (go
to start of body
of loop)
```
The reset statement involves incrementing the counter such as adding one to it and then shifting the pointer arrow back to the top of the loop.

The Exit condition is that if the counter equals (or is greater than, less than, etc.) some value, then the pointer arrow will shift out of the loop.

Note that each time the pointer arrow goes through the loop, the number in the counter is incremented by 1. If the number in the counter is 100 that means that the computer will execute the body of the loop 100 times.

TRY IT

Suppose you have a program to print out squares of a number starting with 2. Your program could be as follows:

```
10   LET X = 2
20   LET X = X * X
30   PRINT X
40   GO TO 20
50   END
```

This program will go indefinitely until it reaches a number too high for the computer to store, or until you use an external command (see Appendix) to stop it. Modify this program so that it will print out just the first six values for X.

In order to accomplish this goal you can use a waiting-for-a-counter loop. Line 5 is added to set a counter to 0; line 35 is added to increment the counter for each time the pointer arrow goes through the loop, and line 40 is added to have the program branch outside the loop to the END if the loop has been executed six times.

```
 5   LET C = 0
10   LET X = 2
20   LET X = X * X
30   PRINT X
35   LET C = C + 1
40   IF C < 6 THEN 10
50   END
```

The output will be these numbers: 4, 16, 256, 65536, 4.29496E09, 1.84467E19, with each number printed in a separate line. (Remember that the E means scientific notation.)

TRY IT

What will be the output of the following program?

```
10   LET C = 0
20   READ X
30   DATA 100
35   PRINT X
40   LET X = X/2
45   LET C = C +1
50   IF C < 8 THEN 35
99   END
```

_____

_____

_____

_____

The output will be as follows:

```
100
50
25
12.5
6.25
3.125
1.5625
.78125
.340625
```

Notice that the computer will get to line 50 eight times, but when the counter is increased to 9 the computer will shift to line 99 and stop.

PROGRAM QUIZ

In this chapter you have learned about four different configurations involving the IF and GO TO statement. The branching configuration was presented in chapter 4, and was expanded in this chapter. In addition, three looping configurations were presented (Repeating a READ-in, Waiting for a Data Number, and Waiting for a Counter). Each of these configurations share the characteristics of having an initial condition, an exit condition (or decision condition), a body of the loop, and a reset instruction. For each of the examples given below, state in English how each of the four characteristics is involved and tell which statements correspond to each of these four characteristics. Also, for each, list the lines that the pointer arrow will point to, in order.

```
(1) 10   READ F
    20   DATA 1, 2, 3, 4
    30   LET M = .31 * F
    40   PRINT F, M
    50   GO TO 10
    60   END
```

Initial condition: _____

Exit condition: _____

Body of the loop: _____

Reset: _____

Lines that the pointer arrow points to: _____

Initial condition. Four numbers (1, 2, 3, 4) are waiting at the input window, and the first one (1) is read into memory space F. This is indicated by lines 10 and 20.

Exit condition. When the computer tries to read in a number but there are no numbers waiting in line at the input window, the computer will stop and write "OUT OF DATA." This will occur after 4 has been read into space F. This is indicated in line 10.

Body of the loop. This contains a LET statement and a PRINT statement, in lines 30 and 40.

Reset. At line 50, the GO TO statement brings the pointer arrow back up to the starting point.

Lines. 10, 20, 30, 40, 50,10, 20, 30, 40, 50, 10, 20, 30, 40, 50, 10, 20, 30, 40, 50, 10. (Here the computer tries to read in the next data card but there is none.)

```
(2) 10   READ C
    20   DATA 0, 10, 20, 30
    30   IF C > 22.22 THEN 50
    40   PRINT "ITS COLD", C
    45   GO TO 10
    50   PRINT "ITS HOT", C
    60   GO TO 10
    70   END
```

Initial condition: _____
Decision condition: _____
Body of the loop: _____
Reset: _____
Lines that the pointer arrow points to: _____

_____

Initial condition. Four numbers are waiting in line at the input window and the first one (0) is read into memory space C. This is indicated by the READ and DATA statements on lines 10 and 20.

Decision Condition. The decision occurs at line 30 for the IF statement. Here the computer decides whether to follow branch 1 (consisting of line 40) or branch 2 (consisting of line 50). There is also the same exit condition as in the previous example since the READ statement at line 10 will result in an exit from both loops when the data run out.

Body of the loop. The body of loop 1 is the PRINT statement in line 40. The body of loop 2 is the PRINT statement in line 50.

Reset. The system is reset by the GO TO statements at either line 60 or line 45. At this point the pointer returns to the start of the program.

Lines. 10, 20, 30, 40, 45, 10, 20, 30, 40, 45, 10, 20, 30, 40, 45, 10, 20, 30 (here C is greater than 22.22), 50, 60, 10 (here the computer runs out of data).

```
(3) 10   READ F
    20   DATA 1, 2, 3, 4, .9999
    30   IF F = .9999 THEN 90
    40   LET M = .31 * F
    50   PRINT F, M
    60   GO TO 10
    90   END
```

Initial condition: _____

Exit condition: _____

Body of the loop: _____

Reset: _____

Lines that the pointer arrow will point to: _____

_____

Initial condition. In this example, five numbers are waiting at the input window (1, 2, 3, 4, .9999), and the first one is read into memory space F. This is indicated in lines 10 and 20.

Exit condition. The IF statement on line 30 provides a decision that allows the computer to shift out of the loop.

Body of the loop. The LET and PRINT statements on lines 40 and 50 are the operations that are repeated for each loop.

Reset. The GO TO statement at line 60 allows the system to reset back to line 10.

Lines. 10, 20, 30, 40, 50, 60, 10, 20, 30, 40, 50, 60, 10, 20, 30, 40, 50, 60, 10, 20, 30, 40, 50, 60, 10, 20 (here .9999 is read in), 30 (here the match is made), 90.

```
(4) 10   LET C = 0
    20   READ X
    30   DATA 100
    35   PRINT X
    40   LET X = X/2
    45   LET C = C + 1
    50   IF C < 3 THEN 35
    99   END
```

Initial condition: _____

Exit condition: _____

Body of the loop: _____

Reset: _____

Lines that the pointer arrow will point to: _____

_____

Initial condition: The counter is at 0 (line 10), and the number 100 has been read into memory space X (at lines 20 and 30).

Exit condition. When the value in the counter is equal to 3, then the pointer arrow will shift out of the loop to line 99. This decision occurs at line 50 in the IF statement.

Body of the loop. In the body of the loop a number is divided by 2 and printed out (lines 35 and 40) and a counter is incremented (line 45).

Reset. At line 50, the pointer arrow is shifted back to the start of the loop.

Lines. 10, 20, 30, 35, 40, 45, 50, 10, 20, 30, 35, 40, 45, 50, 10, 20, 30, 35, 40, 45 (now counter equals 3), 50 (now the exit condition is met), 99.

Summary

You have learned how to use the IF and GO TO statements to turn your program into a looping program. As you can see, the computer system has a great advantage over our pocket calculator—you need give the instructions only once to the computer, but on your calculator you must go through each step even if you are just repeating what you have done before.

Let us return to the gradebook problem discussed in the Summary of chapter 4. In this program, three exam grades are given for a student (Sam) and the program determines his average and grade.

```
 10    READ E1, E2, E3
 20    DATA 95, 85, 75
 30    LET A = (E1 + E2 + E3)/3
 40    PRINT "FOR SAM"
 60    PRINT "EXAM 1 SCORE IS" E1
 70    PRINT "EXAM 2 SCORE IS" E2
 80    PRINT "EXAM 3 SCORE IS" E3
 90    PRINT "AVERAGE SCORE IS" A
100    IF A > = 70 THEN 120
110    PRINT "NOT PASSING"
115    GO TO 999
120    IF A > = 80 THEN 140
130    PRINT "GRADE IS C"
135    GO TO 999
140    IF A > = 90 THEN 160
150    PRINT "GRADE IS B"
155    GO TO 999
160    PRINT "GRADE IS A"
999    END
```

Suppose that we have more grades for other students. How can we use this program to compute these other grades and averages? We could just copy the first 17 statements (with new line numbers) for each new student. That is similar to the procedure on a pocket calculator. Can you think of a way to use a repeating-a-READ-in loop to turn this program into one that recycles?

Let's assume another student, Sue, scored 80, 90, and 95 on her exams. To add Sue's data we must change the Data statement:

```
 20    DATA 95, 85, 75, 80, 90, 95
```

Further, we should erase line 40 since we want this to be a program for any student. In order to make the program loop, we need to change the GO TO statements and also add one for each branch:

```
115   GO TO 10
135   GO TO 10
155   GO TO 10
165   GO TO 10
```

Now each branch recycles back to the READ statement at line 10.

What will be the output of our revised program? First it will go through lines 10, 20, 30, 60, 70, 80, 90, 100, 120, 140, 150, 155, and then back to 10. On this trip the computer will print the following:

```
EXAM 1 SCORE IS  95
EXAM 2 SCORE IS  85
EXAM 3 SCORE IS  75
AVERAGE SCORE IS 85
GRADE IS B
```

On the next cycle the computer will go through all of the same steps:

```
EXAM 1 SCORE IS  80
EXAM 2 SCORE IS  90
EXAM 3 SCORE IS  95
AVERAGE SCORE IS 88.3333333
GRADE IS B
```

Then the pointer arrow will move from line 155 to 10, but since there is no more data it will print "OUT OF DATA."

Let's suppose that you have a class of 20 students, each with 3 exam scores. You could convert the gradebook program into one that used a waiting-for-a-counter loop. When the loop reached above 20, it would be time to stop. How would you convert the program?

First, you would have to set a counter to zero.

```
5   LET C = 0
```

Then you would need to expand your DATA statement or use more DATA statements to contain all the scores (60 in all).

```
20   DATA 95, 85, 75, 80, 90, 95   and so on
```

Next you could direct all the branches to the same point in the program by changing the GO TO statements:

```
115   GO TO 200
135   GO TO 200
155   GO TO 200
```

At line 200, the counter could be incremented and then a exit test made:

```
200    LET C = C + 1
210    IF C <= 20 THEN 10
```

In this case, the computer will determine the average and grade for the first 20 sets of three scores. However, after the 20th cycle, the counter will be incremented to 21 (at line 200) and the exit condition will be met (at line 210), so the pointer arrow will move to line 999 and the program will end.

6

Advanced Looping

Overview
FOR and NEXT Statements
FOR and NEXT in a Waiting-for-a-Counter Loop
Summary

Overview

This chapter shows how you can use the FOR and NEXT statements instead of the IF and GO TO (and LET) statements to form loops. The FOR and NEXT statements provide a short way of telling the computer to make loops like those you learned about in Chapter 5. If you feel that you already have learned plenty about looping programs in Chapter 5, you can skip this chapter without losing any continuity in this book. As you can see, you have come to a branch in this book: if you want to learn about a shorter way to form loops, read this chapter; if not, you can just go on to Chapter 7.

The FOR and NEXT statements are especially helpful when you have many loops in a program; they make your program easier to read. This chapter uses the same ideas as the previous chapter, though it does focus on the waiting-for-a-counter loop.

For example, in our unit price problem, we might have a long list of data: a 12-ounce jar costs $1.03, a 7-ounce jar costs 66¢, a 9.5-ounce jar costs 79¢, and so on. Let's suppose that we have data from 100 products listed in our DATA statement. In order to get the first 25 unit prices printed out, we could add lines 5, 97 and 98 to our program.

```
 5   LET C = 1
10   READ T, N
20   DATA 103, 12, 66, 7, 79, 9.5 AND SO ON
30   LET U = T/N
40   PRINT "TOTAL COST IS" T
60   PRINT "NUMBER OF OUNCES IS" N
80   PRINT "UNIT COST IS" U
90   IF U > = 10 THEN 97
95   PRINT "THATS CHEAP"
97   LET C = C + 1
98   IF C < = 25 THEN 10
99   END
```

In this case, the computer will compute values for the first 25 unit prices (using 50 numbers from DATA statement). Notice that line 5 initializes the counter. This means that the counter is set to its initial value—in this case, the value is 1. Line 97 increments it each time a new unit price is computed, and line 98 presents a decision (to go to the END if 25 computations have been computed).

The same output can be generated using FOR and NEXT statements. Line 5 would be changed:

```
 5   FOR C = 1 TO 25
```

Lines 97 and 98 would be changed:

```
97   NEXT C
```

Each time the pointer arrow reaches line 97, the counter is increased by 1. The arrow will jump back up to the line with FOR (line 5) as long as the value in C is between 1 and 25. Thus we can use the statements from Chapter 5 or we can use the FOR and NEXT statements to create a waiting-for-a-counter loop. The advantage to FOR and NEXT is that they are easier for you to read and will help later when you get into advanced BASIC.

FOR and NEXT Statements

In the previous chapter you learned how to produce four common types of loops. In this chapter you will learn about a shortcut way to make loops, especially for the waiting-for-a-counter loop. The FOR and NEXT statements accomplish exactly the same goal as the format of the counter set LET, IF, GO TO, and formula LET statements you learned about in the previous chapter. Exactly the same operations can be performed in the computer. However, the FOR and NEXT statements have an advantage over other loop-writing methods because they require you to write less. They help make your programs shorter. They also take care of the counter process automatically.

The FOR and NEXT statements need each other. You cannot have one without the other. The FOR statement must come first in a program, followed by other lines, and eventually followed by a NEXT statement. Whenever you see a FOR there must be a corresponding NEXT somewhere below it in the program; whenever you see a NEXT there must be a corresponding FOR somewhere above it.

Since you already know about many statements, let's take a moment to show how the FOR and NEXT statements are really just the same as statements you already know about.

The **FOR statement** is really shorthand for two statements, a counter set statement such as

```
LET C = 0
```

and an IF statement such as

```
IF  C = 100  THEN  90
```

Thus the FOR statement sets a counter to a value, and tells the computer the exit condition for leaving the loop.

The **NEXT statement** is also shorthand for two statements, a counter increment LET, such as

```
LET C = C + 1
```

and a GO TO statement that allows the computer to reset back to start of the loop (i.e., the line of the FOR statement).

In short, you can translate the FOR and NEXT as follows:

FOR statement means:

Counter Set LET (Set a counter to a value)
Exit condition IF (Jump to the line after the NEXT statement if the exit condition exists)

NEXT statement means:

Counter Increment LET (Increment a counter by a certain value)
Reset GO TO (Reset the system by moving the pointer arrow back
to the FOR statement)

We will now look at the FOR and NEXT statements in more
detail, but it will help you if you remember that the FOR statement is
just like a LET and an IF, while the NEXT statement is just like a LET
and a GO TO.

The format of the FOR statement is

line
number   FOR   address
name = number or address name TO number or address name STEP number or address name

where a line number goes in the first blank, an address name goes in
the first blank after FOR, a number or address name goes in the blank
after the equals sign, a number or address name goes in the blank
after TO, and a number or address name goes in the blank after STEP.
The STEP and its blank may be omitted, as follows:

line
number FOR address name = number or address name TO number or address name

in which case the STEP is assumed to be 1.

The format of the NEXT statement is

line
number NEXT address name

where the line number that goes in the blank must be greater than
the line number for a FOR statement that came earlier in the program, and the address name must be the same as the one used in the
corresponding FOR statement. Thus every time there is a FOR statement, there must be a corresponding NEXT statement somewhere
later in the program, with the same address name. The line of the
FOR statement is the beginning boundary for the loop and the line of
the NEXT statement is the ending boundary. Thus all statements in
between the FOR and NEXT statement are in the body of the loop.

For the statements

```
10   FOR X = 1 TO 5 STEP 2
20   NEXT X
```

the following condition exists in the computer before the FOR
statement is executed:

▶ *There is a certain value in memory space X (this is the counter).*

After the FOR statement has been executed, the computer is in the following state:

▶ *If the certain value in memory space X (the counter) is more than 5, the computer will have moved directly to the statement below line 20. If the number in the counter is 5 or less, then the computer will be working on the statement just below line 10. If this is the first time the computer has come to line 10, the number 1 will now be in space X, and the computer will be working on the statement just below line 10.*

The conditions in the computer before the NEXT statement is executed are as follows:

▶ *The value in memory space X (the counter) is 5 or less; this allowed the computer to execute the statements in the body of the loop. All the statements in the body of the loop have been executed.*

The conditions in the computer after the NEXT statement has been executed are as follows:

▶ *The value in the counter has been increased by the STEP size; in this case the value in memory space X has been increased by 2. The pointer arrow has been moved back up to the FOR statement at line 10.*

For the statements

```
10   FOR X = 1 TO 5 STEP 2
20   NEXT X
```

the operations for the FOR statement are as follows:

1. Find memory space X; this is the counter.
2. If this is the first time at line 10, erase the number in X and put in 1 (just like a counter set LET); otherwise retain whatever number is in X.
3. Compare the number in the counter to 5 (the exit condition).
4. If the number in the counter is 5 or less (i.e., the exit condition is not met), then move the pointer arrow to the line just below line 10 and start working on the body of the loop.
5. If the number in the counter is greater than 5, move the pointer arrow to the line directly below the NEXT statement, ignoring all statements in between.

The operations entailed in the NEXT statement are as follows:

1. Find memory space X; this space is serving as a counter for this statement.
2. Add the STEP size (in this case, 2) to the value in the counter.
3. Destroy the old number in the counter.
4. Put in the new sum at the counter.
5. Move the pointer arrow back up to the FOR statement at line 10.

You should also note the many "invisible" statements in a FOR and NEXT loop. In the statements

```
10   FOR X = 1 TO 5 STEP 2
20   NEXT X
```

there are the following invisible statements:

1. The FOR statement means to set the counter to 1 when the loop is begun. Thus the FOR statement tells the computer, "LET X = 1." This counter set LET is executed only on the first time that the computer comes to line 10.
2. The FOR statement also contains an IF statement. Note that if the value in X is greater than 5 the pointer arrow should shift to the next line after the NEXT statement. Thus the FOR statement tells the computer, "IF X > 5 THEN" (go to next line after 20).
3. The NEXT statement means to add a number to the counter. Thus NEXT involves a formula LET statement such as "LET X = X + 2."
4. The NEXT statement also involves an invisible GO TO statement. In this case, NEXT means, "GO TO 10."

Once you realize that FOR and NEXT contain these four invisible statements, you will see that FOR and NEXT are just shortcut ways to tell the computer to loop.

TRY IT

Suppose the following statements were in a program:

```
10
20   FOR X = 1 TO 5
30
40
50   NEXT  X
60
```

If you wanted to accomplish the same operations using LET, IF, and

GO TO statements, tell how you would rewrite the statements at lines 20 and 50.

```
10 _____
20 _____
   _____
30 _____
40 _____
50 _____
   _____
55 _____
60 _____
```

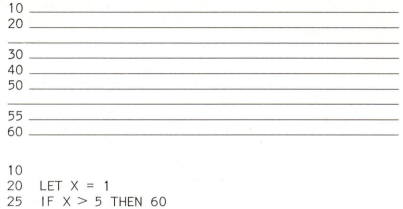

```
10
20    LET X = 1
25    IF X > 5 THEN 60
30
40
50    LET X = X + 1
55    GO TO 25
60
```

Note that the FOR statement can be rewritten as a LET statement (to set a counter) and an IF statement (to specify the exit condition); the NEXT statement can be rewritten as a LET statement (to increment the counter) and a GO TO statement (to reset the loop).

A better system would be:

```
10
20    LET X = 1
30
40
50    LET X + 1
50    LET X = X + 1
55    IF X < = 5 THEN 30
60
```

TRY IT

Suppose the following statements were in a program:

```
10
20    FOR X = 1 TO 5 STEP 2
30
40
50    NEXT X
60
```

List the lines that the pointer arrow will point to until it reaches line 60. _____

_____

_____

_____

_____

_____

The lines will be: 10, 20 (counter is set to 1), 30, 40, 50 (counter is incremented to 3), 30, 40, 50 (counter is incremented to 5) 30, 40, 50, 60. Thus there are three loops back from line 50 to 30.

FOR and NEXT in a Waiting-for-a-Counter Loop

Let's see how you can use the FOR and NEXT statements to form a waiting-for-a-counter loop. In this configuration, the computer executes the loop until a counter reaches a certain value. Each time the loop is executed, a counter is incremented. When the counter reaches a certain value, the pointer arrow will shift outside the loop to a lower part of the program.

The format of this type of loop is as follows:

`FOR C = _____ TO _____`	The initial condition is that the counter is set to some value (such as 1).
	The exit condition is that the counter does not contain a number between the two indicated in the FOR statement. If not, the pointer arrow will shift to the statement below the NEXT statement.
`Body of loop`	The body of the loop may contain statements such as LET and PRINT, etc.

`NEXT C`
`Rest of program`
`END`
	The reset instruction is to increment the counter by the STEP size and then automatically to go back to the line with FOR on it.

Note that each time the pointer arrow goes through the loop, the number in the counter is incremented by whatever the STEP size is (i.e., the number in the blank after STEP).

As an example, consider the following program:

```
10   PRINT "THIS IS A LOOPING PROGRAM"
20   FOR C = 1 TO 5
30   READ X
40   DATA 2, 3, 6, 4, 8, 10, 5, 15
50   PRINT X
60   NEXT C
80   END
```

This program will print out the first five numbers waiting in line at the input window. First, the counter is set to 1. Next, the counter passes the test so, the first number in line (2) is read into space X, and then it is printed. At line 60, the counter is reset to 2, and the pointer arrow is shifted back up to line 20. After 8 is printed, the counter will be incremented from 5 to 6. Then the pointer arrow will move to line 20; since the counter now meets the exit condition (i.e., it is greater than 5), the arrow will shift to the line below NEXT, which is line 80. The program will stop.

The initial condition is that the counter is set at 1. The exit condition is that the counter is not equal to a value between 1 and 5. The body of the loop is to read and print. The reset statement is handled by NEXT; the counter is incremented and the arrow is shifted to line 20.

TRY IT

Suppose you have written the following waiting-for-a-counter program:

```
20   READ X
30   DATA 100
40   FOR C = 0 TO 7
50   PRINT X
60   LET X = X/2
70   NEXT C
80   END
```

Change this program so that it accomplishes the same goal but uses LET, IF, and GO TO statements instead of FOR and NEXT.

_____

_____

_____

_____

_____

_____

```
20   READ X
30   DATA 100
35   LET C = 0
50   PRINT X
60   LET X = X/2
65   LET C = C + 1
70   IF C < 8 THEN 50
80   END
```

There are several different ways to arrange the statements; however, in each case the FOR statement is replaced by a counter set LET while the NEXT statement is replaced by a counter increment LET and an IF statement.

TRY IT

What will be the output of the following program?

```
20   READ X
30   DATA 100
40   FOR C = 0 TO 7
50   PRINT X
60   LET X = X/2
70   NEXT C
80   END
```

What lines will the pointer arrow point to?

_____

_____

_____

The computer will make eight trips through the body of the loop and will perform the PRINT (line 50) and the LET (line 60) on each. Thus there will be eight numbers printed out, as follows:

```
100
50
25
12.5
6.25
3.125
1.5625
.78125
```

The pointer arrow will point to: 20, 30, 40, 50, 60, 70, then 40 through 70 for seven more times, then 80.

PROGRAM QUIZ

(1) You should now be proficient in building waiting-for-a-counter loops using the shortcut statements FOR and NEXT. As you learned earlier, each loop program you write has the following characteristics: initial condition, exit condition, body of the loop, reset. Write a program to print out a number and its square for the first 100 whole numbers, using the FOR and NEXT statements.

One way to accomplish this goal is as follows:

```
10    FOR X = 1 TO 100
20    LET Y = X * X
30    PRINT X, Y
40    NEXT X
50    END
```

Note that in this case we are using the memory space X both as a counter and as something to print out.

(2) Suppose you have written the following program:

```
10   FOR X = 1 TO 100
20   LET Y = X * X
30   PRINT X, Y
40   NEXT X
50   END
```

What are the four characteristics of the loop? Which statements relate to each one?

Initial Condition: _____

Exit Condition: _____

Body of the Loop: _____

Reset: _____

_____

The characteristics and corresponding statements are as follows:

Initial Condition. The number 1 is in memory space X. This is indicated in the FOR statement.

Exit Condition. When the number 100 is in memory space X, this indicates that the last loop has arrived. The statement corresponding to this condition is the FOR (and NEXT).

Body. The formula LET (at line 20) and the PRINT at line (30) constitute the body of the loop.

Reset. The NEXT statement allows the pointer arrow to move back up to line 10.

(3) Suppose you wanted to modify the following program so that it would print out the first 100 positive even numbers, each with its square. How would you change this program?

```
10   FOR X = 1 TO 100
20   LET Y = X * X
30   PRINT X, Y
40   NEXT X
50   END
```

_____

_____

_____

_____

_____

```
10   FOR X = 2 TO 200 STEP 2
20   LET Y = X * X
30   PRINT X, Y
40   NEXT X
50   END
```

Only the FOR statement is changed! The STEP size is now set at 2, and the range is set from 2 to 200. An alternative is as follows:

```
10   FOR X = 1 TO 100 .
20   LET A = 2 * X
30   LET B = A ↑ 2
40   PRINT A, B
50   NEXT X
60   END
```

Summary

You should now see how you can make a waiting-for-a-counter loop in either of two ways: using LET, IF, and GO TO or using the FOR and NEXT statements. Let's apply the shortcut FOR-NEXT loop to our gradebook problem. Suppose that you, as an instructor, have three exam scores for each of 20 students in your class. You would like a program to find averages and grades for each of the 20 students.

In Chapter 5 you learned how to make a waiting-for-a-counter loop such as the following:

```
  5   LET C = 1
 10   READ E1, E2, E3
 20   DATA 95, 85, 75, 80, 90, 95 for 18 more students
 30   LET A = (E1 + E2 + E3)/3
 60   PRINT "EXAM 1 SCORE IS" E1
 70   PRINT "EXAM 2 SCORE IS" E2
 80   PRINT "EXAM 3 SCORE IS" E3
 90   PRINT "AVERAGE SCORE IS" A
100 ⎫
160 ⎭ lines 100 to 160 select the grade, as on p. 75
200   LET C = C + 1
210   IF C <= 20 THEN 10
999   END
```

As you can see, this program is quite long, and there are many places (in lines 100 to 160) where there are jumps. To make the loop in this

program more obvious (i.e., easier for you to read) we could use the
FOR and NEXT statements. Instead of line 5, the statement would be

```
5   FOR C = 1 TO 20
```

and lines 200 and 210 would be replaced with the following statement:

```
200   NEXT C
```

Using the FOR and NEXT statements makes it clearer that the body
of the loop runs between lines 5 and 200.

The FOR-NEXT method of writing loops is particularly helpful
when there are many loops in your program. Let's suppose that you
wanted to improve further on your program by reading in only one
exam score at a time. You could change lines 10, 20, and 30 as
follows:

```
 8   LET T = 0
10   FOR X = 1 TO 3
15   READ E
20   DATA 95, 85, 75, 80, 90, 95   and so on
25   LET T = T + E
27   NEXT X
30   LET A = T/3
```

The loop between lines 10 and 27 reads in a DATA number, adds it to
the previous numbers read in, and then repeats this until three numbers have been read in. Note that the counter T must be initialized in
line 8, and that the LET statement at line 30 must be revised.

When we insert this loop into a larger loop, we generate the
following program:

```
  5   FOR C = 1 TO 20
  8   LET T = 0
 10   FOR X = 1 TO 3
 15   READ E
 20   DATA 95, 85, 75, 80, 90, 95 and so on
 23   PRINT "EXAM IS" E
 25   LET T = T + E
 27   NEXT X
 30   LET A = T/3
 90   PRINT  "AVERAGE SCORE IS" A
100
      lines 100 to 160 select the grade, as on p. 75
160
200   NEXT C
999   END
```

Note that the loop between lines 10 and 27 (for finding three exam scores and determining the total) fits within the larger loop between lines 5 and 200 (for finding the average and grade for each person). Thus you know that the body of the loop between lines 10 and 27 will be executed three times for each student, or a total of 60 times in this program. Do you think that the FOR and NEXT statements help you read this program?

7

Interactive Programs

Overview

So far we have added more memory to our computer, simplified instructions for computations, and allowed it to make jumps. However, note that you must put all the data into the computer at the start (in your DATA statement) and then the program is run. One modification that would be useful in some cases would be to allow the user to interact with the program as it runs. In this chapter you will learn about the INPUT statement as a way of writing programs

interactive mode *in the interactive mode.*

For example, in our unit price problem, the computer could ask you to give the total cost and number of ounces from the keyboard, and then it would compute the unit price. In this revised example, the program would look like this:

```
10   INPUT "TOTAL COST" T
20   INPUT "NUMBER OF OUNCES" N
30   LET U = T/N
40   PRINT "TOTAL COST IS" T
60   PRINT "NUMBER OF OUNCES IS" N
80   PRINT "UNIT COST IS" U
90   IF U ≥ 10 THEN 97
95   PRINT "THATS CHEAP"
97   GO TO 10
99   END
```

In this case the screen would show:

```
TOTAL COST?
```

Then the user might type in 103. The screen would then show:

```
NUMBER OF OUNCES?
```

Then the user might type in 12. The screen would then show:

```
TOTAL COST IS 103
NUMBER OF OUNCES IS 12
UNIT COST IS 8.5833333
THATS CHEAP
```

And then when the computer shifted back up to line 10, the same process could be repeated. Thus in this chapter you will learn how to write and interpret programs involving input from the keyboard.

Interacting with a Running Program

So far we have dealt with programs that require all the data at the start. You simply insert them into the program list space, and the computer executes the program. However, there are also statements that allow you to interact with the computer *while* it is running a program. To understand how you can interact with the computer while it is running, you need to picture yourself sitting at a computer terminal. In front of you is a keyboard (much like a typewriter keyboard) and a screen (much like a TV screen). Messages from the computer are printed on the screen. Also, every message that you type on the keyboard will be printed on the screen. The keyboard gives you another route into the computer (in addition to the input window). What you write on the keyboard (and thus see on the screen) is a message from you to the computer.

In a noninteractive program, you will key in RUN and watch the computer do the rest. (The RUN command is explained in the Appendix.) In an interactive program, the computer will ask you to enter information from the keyboard when it comes to a particular line on its program that contains an INPUT statement. Thus when the pointer arrow on the program list comes to this statement, the computer will wait for you to type something on the keyboard. In this way you can interact with a running program.

Earlier you learned how to get data from the outside world into the computer's memory by using READ and DATA statements. Remember that the DATA statement tells the computer which numbers are lined up at the input window, and the READ statement tells the computer to process the numbers waiting at the window. In this chapter you will learn that there is another way to accomplish the task of taking information from the outside world and putting it into the computer. By using the INPUT statement you can interact with the computer while it is running a program. When it comes to an INPUT statement while running a program, the computer will stop and print a question mark on the output screen; then it will wait until you type in the data from the keyboard. Thus the INPUT statement is a new way of putting data into the computer's memory.

In terms of what is going on inside the computer, you should assume that there is a set of lights in the computer next to the program list. When the RUN light is on, the computer has control of the situation and is executing the statements in order. When the WAIT light is on, the computer is not in control; the user is in control and the computer is waiting for the user to enter some information from the keyboard. When the computer comes to an INPUT statement, the RUN light will go off and the WAIT light will go on; then, when the user types in and presses the return key, the WAIT light will go off and the RUN light will go back on. It is important to keep track of who is in control: the computer (RUN light on) or the user at the keyboard (WAIT light on).

INPUT Statement

The format of the **INPUT statement** is as follows:

| line number _____ | INPUT | address name _____ |

or

| line number _____ | INPUT | address name _____ , | address name _____ , | address name _____ |

or

| line number _____ | INPUT | "message" _____ | address name _____ , | address name _____ , | address name _____ |

A line number goes in the blank to the left of INPUT, an address name or a list of address names (separated by commas) goes to the right of INPUT, and if desired any alphanumeric message may go in the quotation marks just after INPUT. The message part of the INPUT statement is not standard on all BASICs. If your version doesn't allow for messages in an INPUT statement, you can use a PRINT statement such as the following:

| line number _____ | PRINT | "message" _____ |
| line number _____ | INPUT | address name _____ |

Also note that the message is limited, usually to 72 spaces or less.

The result of the INPUT statement is that a question mark will appear on the screen:

?

(The prompt may be a question mark or some other obvious symbol in your version of BASIC.) The computer is now waiting for the user to "say something" by typing in a number on the keyboard. How will the computer know you are finished? You tell the computer by pressing the return key on the keyboard. Thus the format of the user's response as seen in the screen is as follows:

| "message" _____ | ? | user's input _____ | press return key _____ |

The message and ? are typed by the computer (if there is no message in quotation marks for the INPUT statement, the computer will just print the ?); then the next blank is a number (or list of numbers) that the user types on the keyboard, and then the user presses the return key. Note that the numbers are entered from the keyboard and that they will appear on the screen next to the question mark.

For example, the statement

    10   INPUT T

means that the following conditions exist in the computer prior to the execution of this statement:

> ▶ *There is some unknown number in memory space T and the RUN light is on.*

After this statement has been executed, the following conditions exist:

> ▶ *A question mark has appeared on the user's screen, the user has entered a number and pressed the return key, and that number is now stored in memory space T. Thus the screen has a new line with a ? and a number in it. The RUN light is on again, and the computer has gone on to work on the next statement.*

The screen would look like those in Figure 9 after the INPUT statement.

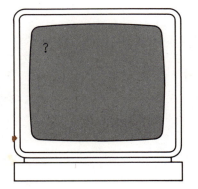 

This is the screen when the pointer arrow gets to line 100, but before the user types anything.

This is the screen after the user has responded and the pointer arrow has gone on to the next statement.

Figure 9

The operations performed for the statement

```
10    INPUT  T
```

are as follows:

1. The computer prints a question mark (?) on the next available line of the output screen.
2. The RUN light is turned off; the WAIT light goes on. (Control shifts to the keyboard.)
3. The user types in a number at the keyboard (e.g., 103).
4. The number is printed on the screen next to the question mark.
5. The user presses the return key.
6. The WAIT light goes off; the RUN light goes back on. (Control shifts back to the computer.)
7. The computer finds memory space T.
8. The computer puts the number that was typed on the screen into memory space T, erasing whatever was there before.
9. The computer goes on to the next statement.

TRY IT

Suppose that two lines of a program read as follows:

```
10    READY  Y
45    DATA   6
```

Modify these lines so that numbers (like 6) may be input from keyboard.

——————   INPUT   ——————————————————

The same results can be obtained by using the statement

```
10    INPUT  Y
```

When the computer asks for a number on the screen (by printing a question mark), you just type in 6. This will accomplish the same result as the READ and DATA statements above.

TRY IT

What operations will be performed when the computer comes to the following?

```
10   INPUT Y
```

1. _____

2. _____

3. _____

4. _____

5. _____

6. _____

7. _____

The operations will be as follows:

1. A question mark is printed on the output screen.
2. The RUN light goes off and the WAIT light goes on.
3. The user types in a number (e.g., 6) and presses the return key.
4. The number is printed on the screen, next to the question mark.
5. The RUN light comes back on and the WAIT light goes off.
6. The computer finds space Y and puts the number (6) in it, erasing whatever was there before.
7. The computer goes on to the next statement.

While you may not have combined the operations exactly as was done in this answer, you should have all the steps indicated.

TRY IT

Suppose you wanted to get the number 8.99 into memory space T1. One way to do this is as follows:

```
10   LET T1 = 8.99
```

Here's another way to accomplish the same goal:

```
10   READ T1
12   DATA 8.99
```

Yet, let's use a third way of getting 8.99 into space T1. Tell how you would accomplish this goal using an INPUT statement.

————   I NPUT   ————————————————

————————————————

To accomplish this goal, first you need to have the following statement in your program:

    10   INPUT T1

Then when the computer executes this statement, it will print a question mark on the screen. This is asking you what number you would like inserted into space T1. All you need to do is type 8.99 and press the return key. Then the computer will put 8.99 into T1, erasing whatever was there before.

More INPUT

So far you have learned how to enter one number at a time through the keyboard. The same INPUT statement can be used for a list of numbers. The format of the multiple INPUT statement is

| line
number
———— | I NPUT | address
name
———— , | address
name
———— , | address
name
———— , | address
name
———— |

where a line number goes in the first blank and address names go in the blanks after INPUT. Any number of address names may be used, but there must be a comma between each pair. Remember, though, that the number is restricted by the size of your computer's memory.

The result of the INPUT statement is that a question mark will appear on the output screen:

    ?

The computer is now waiting for you to type in some numbers. The format for typing is

| number
———— , | number
———— , | number
———— , | number
———— , | number
———— | PRESS
RETURN KEYS |

where each blank is a number, commas separate the numbers, and the last key pressed is the return key. (For each INPUT statement, the computer will accept just one RETURN instruction—because that means to let the computer have control again.)

For example, the statement

```
100  INPUT T, N
```

means that before this statement the following conditions obtain:

▶ *There is a number in memory space T and a number in space N and the RUN light is on.*

After this statement the following conditions obtain:

▶ *The screen has a question mark followed by two numbers (which were entered by the user); the first number is now in memory space T and the second number is now in memory space N. The RUN light is on again, and the computer is working on the next statement.*

The information added to the screen would look like that in Figure 10. (Notice, however, that this form of response is not universal. Many BASICs will query with a question mark on a separate line for *each* address name in the list.)

The operations performed for the statement

```
100   INPUT T, N
```

are as follows:

1. The computer prints a question mark on the screen.

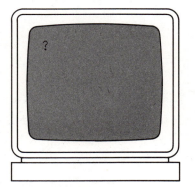

This is the screen when the pointer arrow gets to line 100, but before the user types anything.

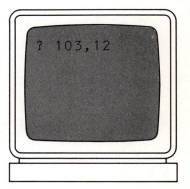

This is the screen after the user has responded and the pointer arrow has gone on to the next statement.

Figure 10

2. The RUN light goes off; the WAIT light goes on. (Control shifts to the keyboard.)
3. The user types in two numbers on the keyboard, separated by a comma (e.g., 103, 12).
4. The numbers are printed on the screen.
5. The user presses the return key.
6. The RUN light goes on; the WAIT light goes off. (Control now shifts to the computer.)
7. The computer finds memory space T and N.
8. The first number (103) is put into space T and the second number (12) is put into space N, erasing whatever was there before.
9. The computer goes on to the next statement.

TRY IT

Suppose that two lines of a program were as follows:

```
30   READ T, Y, Q, X
60   DATA 35, -6.6, 13E2, 15
```

How could you enter these numbers into the corresponding addresses using an INPUT statement, and how would it work?

————————   I NPUT   ————————

First, you would change the READ and DATA statements to one INPUT statement:

```
30   INPUT T, Y, Q, X
```

Then when the computer printed a question mark on the screen, you would type the following after the question mark:

```
?   35, -6.6, 13E2, 15
```

Note that the order in which you type the numbers is important. If you typed

```
?  35, 15, -6.6, 13E2
```

then 35 would go into T, 15 into Y, -6.6 into Q, and 13E2 into X.

TRY IT

Suppose you came to the following line in a program:

```
30   INPUT T, Y, Q, X
```

What operations would occur in the computer and at the keyboard?

_____

_____

_____

_____

_____

_____

Your list should contain the following events:

1. A question mark is printed on the screen.
2. The RUN light goes off and the WAIT light goes on.
3. The user types in four numbers separated by commas (such as 35, -6.6, 13E2, 15), and then presses the return key.
4. The numbers appear on the screen.
5. The RUN light goes back on while the WAIT light goes off.
6. The computer finds spaces T, Y, Q, and X and puts 35 into T, -6.6 into Y, 13E2 into Q, and 15 into X, destroying any previous numbers in these spaces.
7. The computer goes on to the next statement.

TRY IT

Suppose you wanted to put the number 1 into space A, the number 2 into space B, 3 into C, and 4 into D. Using a READ and a DATA statement, you could accomplish this goal as follows:

```
10   READ A, B, C, D
20   DATA 1,2,3,4
```

You could also accomplish this with four LET statements:

```
10   LET  A  =  1
12   LET  B  =  2
14   LET  C  =  3
16   LET  D  =  4
```

However, do it with an INPUT statement.

—————— INPUT ——————————————————

First, you would write an INPUT statement:

```
10   INPUT  A,  B,  C,  D
```

Then when the computer printed a question mark, you could type

```
?  1,  2,  3,  4
```

followed by pressing the return key. An alternative method is as follows:

```
10   INPUT  A
12   INPUT  B
14   INPUT  C
16   INPUT  D
```

However, can you tell how many question marks would be printed on the screen in this case? ————

TRY IT

Suppose the following statements were in a program:

```
10   INPUT  X
20   INPUT  X
```

Further, suppose that the user types in his age (21) for the first question mark, and his height (62) for the second question mark. What number will be in space X after both statements have been executed?

_____ If you wanted to retain both numbers in memory, what could you do?

_____ INPUT _____

_____ INPUT _____

The answer is 62. For the first INPUT, the computer will put 21 into space, erasing whatever was there before. Then when it executes the second INPUT statement, it will put 62 into space X, erasing the previous number (21). In order to retain both numbers, you could use two different address names such as X for line 10 and Y for line 20.

INPUT with a Message

To cue the user about what numbers should be entered, quotation marks can be used with the INPUT statement. The format is

line number	INPUT	"message"	address name	address name	address name
_____		_____	_____ ,	_____ ,	_____

where a line number goes to the left of INPUT, the message goes in the quotes, and a list of one or more address names goes to the right of the quotes.

For example, the statement

```
10   INPUT "TOTAL COST (IN CENTS)" T
```

has the following conditions before it is executed:

▶ _Some unknown number is in memory space T._

After this statement, the computer is in the following state:

▶ _The output screen has a message, "TOTAL COST (IN CENTS)" followed by a question mark on it, and there is a number on the screen after the question mark (that the user has entered). The number is in memory space T._

The screen would appear as in Figure 11.

This is the screen when the
pointer arrow gets to line 100,
but before the user types anything.

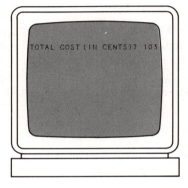

This is the screen after the
user has responded and the
pointer arrow has gone on to
the next statement.

Figure 11

The statement

    10   INPUT "TOTAL COST (IN CENTS)" T

means that the following operations are performed:

1. The computer prints the message "TOTAL COST IN CENTS"
   and a question mark (?) on the next line of the screen.
2. The RUN light goes off, the WAIT light goes on. (Control
   shifts to the keyboard.)
3. The user types in a number.
4. The number is printed on the screen.
5. The user presses the return key.
6. The RUN light goes on; the WAIT light goes off. (Control
   shifts to the computer.)
7. The computer finds memory space T.
8. The first number (103) is put into T, erasing whatever was
   there before.
9. The computer goes on to the next statement.

TRY IT

Suppose you wanted to store the user's year of birth. Write an INPUT statement that would ask for the user's year of birth and store the answer in memory space Y.

———————   INPUT   —————————————————————————

This could be accomplished as follows:

10   INPUT "TYPE IN YOUR YEAR OF BIRTH AND THEN PRESS THE RETURN KEY" Y

In this case the user would see the message on the screen followed by a question mark.

STOP Command

Suppose that you run out of data so that you have nothing to input when the question mark comes on the screen. You cannot just leave because the computer is waiting for you to "say something." There are two ways to stop the program. One is to enter **STOP** into the keyboard, followed by pressing the return key. Another technique that will accomplish the same goal (on most systems) is to press down the letter C and the control key at the same time. (The technique for ending a program with INPUT depends partly on the characteristics of your terminal.)

Before you write STOP and press the return key, the computer is in the following state:

▶ *A question mark has been printed on the screen, and the computer is waiting for you to enter a message.*

After the STOP command, the following state occurs:

▶ *The computer has stopped waiting for a number and will print out "READY" on the screen to let you know that another program may be started. (Some BASICs may say "DONE" rather than "READY.")*

The operations performed for the STOP command are as follows:

1. Stop waiting for a number to be entered.
2. Print out "READY" on the screen.
3. Now the computer is ready to go on with another program or repeat the one that was just stopped.

TRY IT

Suppose you are writing a program that will compute gas mileage. As part of the program you want the user to type in the odometer reading at the start of the trip (this number will be stored in memory space S) and the odometer reading at the finish of the trip (this number will be stored in space F). Can you write INPUT statements that will handle the odometer readings?

——— INPUT ———————

——— INPUT ———————

```
10   INPUT "PUT YOUR ODOMETER READING AT THE START" S
20   INPUT "PUT YOUR ODOMETER READING AT THE FINISH" F
```

In this case, the first number that your user types in will go in space S. The second number will go in space F.

TRY IT

What operations will be performed for the following statements?

```
10   INPUT "ODOMETER READING AT START"
20   INPUT "ODOMETER READING AT FINISH" S, F
```

———————————————

———————————————

———————————————

———————————————

An error message will appear on your screen since you have an INPUT statement without any address names for it at line 10. At line 20 you request just one number but the computer is expecting two and will wait until you enter the second one. In some cases it might assign a zero to the second name (F) or it might give you another error message.

TRY IT

Suppose you walk up to a friend who is working at an output screen. You see the following information on the screen.

```
?   STOP
READY
```

What does this tell you?

_____

_____

_____

_____

One possibility is that the program came to an INPUT statement—this is indicated by the "?" on the screen. Then the user wanted to exit from this program so he typed in "STOP"—this is indicated by the "STOP" that was typed on the screen by the user. Then the computer put away the program and is now ready for any new program to be inserted into its program space—this is indicated by the "READY" printed by the computer.

PROGRAM QUIZ

(1) Now that you learned about INPUT statements, you will be amazed to see how many kinds of things you can do. For example, remember the program from the previous chapter's Program Quiz, as follows:

```
10   FOR X = 1 TO 100
20   LET Y = X * X
30   PRINT X, Y
40   NEXT X
50   END
```

Change this program so that it will be an interactive one that prints out messages like "GIVE ME A NUMBER" and "THE SQUARE IS."

_____

_____

_____

_____

_____

One way to do it is with the following program:

```
10   INPUT "GIVE ME A NUMBER" X
20   LET Y = X * X
30   PRINT "THE SQUARE IS" Y
40   GO TO 10
50   END
```

For any number you enter at the keyboard, the computer will print out its square. However, due to the jump at line 40, the program will go on repeating until you enter the word "STOP."

(2) Suppose you want a program that will take temperatures in Fahrenheit and tell you the corresponding value in Celsius. The formula for converting Fahrenheit to Celsius is

$$C = (F-32) * (5/9).$$

Write an interactive program to make the conversions.

_____

_____

_____

_____

_____

_____

```
10    INPUT "WHATS THE TEMPERATURE" F
20    LET C = (F-32) * (5/9)
30    PRINT "THE CELSIUS TEMPERATURE IS" C
40    GO TO 10
50    END
```

In this case, the program will ask for a temperature, then give the Celsius temperature, and then loop back up to line 10 and ask again. The program will loop repeatedly until the user stops it with a command like "STOP."

(3) Suppose you were given a program like this:

```
10    INPUT "WHATS THE TEMPERATURE" F
20    LET C = (F-32) * (5/9)
30    PRINT "THE CELSIUS TEMPERATURE IS" C
40    GO TO 10
50    END
```

What would happen if line 40 was eliminated? _____
What would happen if line 50 was eliminated? _____

_____

If line 40 were eliminated the computer would print a question mark on the screen, wait for the user to type in a number and press the return key; then it would store that number in space F, perform the computation given for the LET statement, print out the result on the output screen (in line 30), and stop. Only one Fahrenheit to Celsius conversion would be possible.

If line 50 were eliminated there might be an error message (depending on your particular computer) and, in some cases, the program would not run.

(4) Suppose the mean for a certain exam is 70 and the standard deviation is 10. To tell how many standard deviations a score is from the mean, the formula is as follows: distance from mean = (your score − 70)/10. Write a program to find how many standard deviations from the mean a score is so that the user can interact with the computer.

_____

_____

_____

_____

_____

A program to accomplish this goal is as follows:

```
10   INPUT "WHAT IS YOUR SCORE" S
20   LET D = (S - 70)/10
30   PRINT "YOU DIFFERED BY" D
40   GO TO 10
50   END
```

In this case the computer will take in a number and tell how many standard deviations from the mean it was, and then will ask for another number, and so on.

(4) How many times will the pointer arrow point to line 10 in the following program? _____

```
10   INPUT "WHAT IS YOUR SCORE" S
20   LET D = (S - 70)/10
30   PRINT "YOU DIFFERED BY" D
40   GO TO 10
50   END
```

What will be on the screen if the user writes that his score was 70?

_____

_____

There is no way to know how many times the pointer arrow will come to line 10. It will point at line 10 the same number of times that the user enters a number. After line 10 is finished, the screen would look like this:

```
WHAT IS YOUR SCORE? 70
```

The 70 is input by the user. After line 30, a new line will be added to the screen:

```
YOU DIFFERED BY 0.000000
```

Summary

In this chapter you learned how to turn your static programs into interactive ones. Interactive programs can be very useful when you do not have all your data ready at the start. Why are interactive programs useful? They are useful because they let you select the values that the computer will work on. For example, if you wrote a program to convert Fahrenheit to Celsius temperatures, you might not want every temperature converted—with an interactive program you could specify the values you wanted converted. Or suppose you wrote a program to determine average monthly mortgage payments for any amount of loan, interest rate, and length of loan. In this case, you might want to just type in the amount, length, and rate, and then have the monthly mortgage be computed and printed out. You can probably think of many cases when an interactive program is useful.

Let's go back to our gradebook program discussed in the Summary of the previous chapters. Remember that we want to assign grades to students based on their performance on three exams. For example, Sam earned 95, 85, and 75 on three exams while Sue earned 80, 90, and 95. The noninteractive program required that all scores be entered as part of the program in a DATA statement, such as in the following program:

```
10    READ E1, E2, E3
20    DATA 95, 85, 75, 80, 90, 95
30    LET A = (E1 + E2 + E3)/3
60    PRINT "EXAM 1 SCORE IS" E1
70    PRINT "EXAM 2 SCORE IS" E2
80    PRINT "EXAM 3 SCORE IS" E3
90    PRINT "AVERAGE SCORE IS" A
100   IF A>=70 THEN 120
110   PRINT "NOT PASSING"
115   GO TO 10
120   IF A >= 80 THEN 140
130   PRINT "GRADE IS C"
135   GO TO 10
140   IF A>=90 THEN 160
150   PRINT "GRADE IS B"
155   GO TO 10
160   PRINT "GRADE IS A"
165   GO TO 10
999   END
```

In this program the lines 10 to 90 calculate the average and print it, while lines 100 to 999 determine which grade to assign. Note that this program will operate on the first set of three numbers, then will jump back up to line 10, then operate on the next set of three numbers. On the next jump back up to the READ statement, there will be no more data so the computer will stop and print "OUT OF DATA."

To give the gradebook keeper more flexibility, this program could be converted into an interactive one. Try to modify the program, using INPUT statements.

The interactive version of the program could use these lines instead of the old lines 10 and 20.

```
10    INPUT "SCORE ON EXAM 1" E1
15    INPUT "SCORE ON EXAM 2" E2
20    INPUT "SCORE ON EXAM 3" E3
```

What advantages would your new program have? You would not have to include all the data as part of the program. If you had some "late" data to add (e.g., from a student who took a make-up exam), that would be no problem. To determine Sam's grade, the dialogue on the screen would look like this:

```
SCORE ON EXAM 1? 95
SCORE ON EXAM 2? 85
SCORE ON EXAM 3? 75
EXAM 1 IS 95
EXAM 2 IS 85
EXAM 3 IS 75
AVERAGE SCORE IS 85
GRADE IS B
```

After this, the computer would again ask:

```
SCORE ON EXAM 1?
```

You could then enter the scores for Sue, or you could stop the program. In the above example, you as the user have typed in the 95, 85, and 75 after the question marks but all else was printed out by the computer. You might think that it is not efficient for the computer to repeat the exam scores; however, this gives you a way of checking to make sure the computer was basing its average on the correct scores.

8

Working with Character Strings

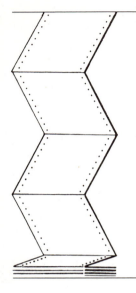

Overview

Let's review the modifications we have made so far for our simple pocket calculator. In Chapter 2 we added more memory spaces; in Chapter 3 we added the ability to perform operations on information in memory spaces; in Chapters 4, 5, and 6 we added the ability to transfer control and make loops in a program; in Chapter 7 we added an interactive option. What else could we possibly need?

So far our computer can store and manipulate numbers only. In this chapter we will introduce the idea that memory spaces can store character strings (non-numbers). Why would it be useful to have memory spaces that hold non-numbers? How would you use them? For example, think of making a mailing list or a program to translate from one language to another. Thus this chapter allows you to use READ, DATA, LET, INPUT, PRINT, and IF statements that involve memory spaces full of characters. Essentially, what must be added to

alphanumeric data *our system is a set of special memory spaces—spaces for alphanumeric data.*

For example, in the unit price problem you might want to keep track of which brand you are dealing with.

```
10    INPUT "BRAND NAME" B$
15    INPUT "TOTAL COST" T
20    INPUT "NUMBER OF OUNCES" N
30    LET U = T/N
35    PRINT B$
40    PRINT "TOTAL COST IS" T
60    PRINT "NUMBER OF OUNCES IS" N
80    PRINT "UNIT COST IS" U
90    IF U ≥ 10 THEN 97
95    PRINT "THATS CHEAP"
97    GO TO 10
99    END
```

In this case, the name of the product is stored in memory space B$ (in line 10) and is printed out in line 35. If the product is Jumbobutter, then that character string will be typed in when the computer asks for it and printed out at the end. The screen would look like this:

```
BRAND NAME? "JUMBOBUTTER"
TOTAL COST? 103
NUMBER OF OUNCES? 12

JUMBOBUTTER
TOTAL COST IS 103
NUMBER OF OUNCES IS 12
UNIT COST IS 8.5833333
THATS CHEAP
```

Then the process would be repeated for a different brand. Note that now you have a record of the product's name along with the unit cost—that's a nice improvement!

Alphanumeric Scoreboard

So far this book has dealt mainly with numbers—how to get them into memory (with READ, LET, and INPUT statements), how to perform arithmetic on numbers (with LET), or how to output numbers from memory (with PRINT). So far we have dealt with memory spaces that could hold only numbers. Now we will introduce a new set of memory spaces, identical to the numerical memory scoreboard, except that this scoreboard can hold character strings—all types of information, such as letters, numbers, and even punctuation marks!

This second memory scoreboard has many spaces just like the numerical scoreboard. However, the address names are different for this scoreboard. The address name can be any single letter, followed by a dollar sign ($) (e.g. A$, B$, C$ . . . so on down to Z$). (Some BASICs also allow any single letter followed by any single digit followed by a dollar sign, such as A1$, A2$, A3$ . . . A0$.) The dollar sign on the address name tells the computer to use the second memory scoreboard—the one for alphanumeric strings.

This scoreboard works exactly like the other one, and you can use all the same statements. It is called the alphanumeric scoreboard because it can hold *any* messages with letters, digits, etc. This means it holds both *alpha*betic and *numeric* information; you *could* use it to hold numbers (like the other scoreboard) or some mixture of characters.

READ and DATA with Alphanumerics

With the alphanumeric scoreboard, you can have any type of message waiting at the input window, and this message can be put into the alphanumeric memory spaces. The format of the program statements is the same as for numbers:

line number	READ	address name	,	address name	,	address name
———		———		———		———

line number	DATA	"message"	,	"message"	,	"message"
———		———		———		———

A line number goes to the left of the READ and a different line number goes to the left of the DATA, alphanumeric address names go in the blanks after the READ, and any combination of words, letters, and symbols can go in each blank after the DATA. Note that the acceptable address names are the same as for number addresses except that each must be followed by a dollar sign ($). There may be any number of addresses given after the READ, but they must be separated by commas. Also note that each message in the DATA statement must be enclosed in quotation marks. (However, some versions of BASIC may not require the quotes.)

For example, a program could contain the following two statements:

```
10 READ B$, S$
20 DATA "JUMBOBUTTER", "MACS GROCERY STORE"
```

Before these statements are executed, the computer is in the following state:

▶ *Unknown messages are in B$ and S$.*

After these statements are executed, the computer is in the following state:

▶ *Memory space B$ contains the message JUMBOBUTTER, and memory space S$ contains the message MACS GROCERY STORE.*

The statements

```
100 READ B$, S$
200 DATA "JUMBOBUTTER", "MACS GROCERY STORE"
```

mean that the following operations will be performed:

1. Line up the messages at the input window in the order, "JUMBOBUTTER," "MACS GROCERY STORE."
2. Erase the messages in memory spaces B$ and S$ (on the alphanumeric memory scoreboard).
3. Move the messages through the input window, reducing the line by two.
4. Put the message "JUMBOBUTTER" in memory space B$, and put the message "MACS GROCERY STORE" in memory space S$.
5. Go on to the next statement.

STYLE BOX: Character String Address Names

digit string

character string

In this chapter you will learn that there are two kinds of memory scoreboards, one that holds only numbers (called **digit string**) and one that holds any message (called **character string**). (Digit strings can include decimal points, negative signs, and scientific notation (E).)

You have already learned about the first type of memory scoreboard. You know that the memory spaces have only certain address names: any of the 26 letters, or any of the 26 letters followed by any single digit. You also know that memory spaces on this scoreboard may hold only digit strings: any number, including a decimal point, a minus sign, or E (for scientific notation).

The second type of memory scoreboard has different rules. The allowable address names are: any of the 26 letters of the alphabet followed by a $ (such as A$, B$ ... Z$). In some BASICs the names can also be any letter followed by any single digit followed by a dollar sign (such as A1$, A2$ ... A0$). Memory spaces can hold any sequence of characters, including strings of digits. Thus any chain of characters including letters, numbers, punctuation marks, etc., may be stored as a character string in the alphanumeric scoreboard.

To make sure you understand these rules, try the following examples. Which of the following are allowable address names for the alphanumeric scoreboard?

```
A1  .N?  AS2$  2A$  $A  B$  "A$"
```

The only allowable address name is B$. The first, second, fifth, and last do not end with $; the third and fourth end with dollar signs but do not contain a single letter or a single letter followed by a single digit.

Which of the following are allowable character strings that could be stored?

```
1235
RIGHT
?$%&!
12 + 12 + 12 = 36
```

Each of the above four strings is allowable in the alphanumeric scoreboard, although only the first (1235) would be allowed for the numeric scoreboard.

TRY IT

What is wrong with these statements, assuming they appear in the same program, and what would you do to correct the problem?

```
10  READ X, Y
20  DATA "YES", "NO"
```

The problem is that non-numeric messages are lined up at the input window, but the computer was asked to store information in the numeric memory spaces only. To correct this problem, the address names in the READ statement should be changed to indicate that the other memory scoreboard is being used:

```
10   READ X$, Y$
20   DATA "YES", "NO"
```

LET with Alphanumerics

You may also use a counter set LET to put alphanumeric information into the alphanumeric scoreboard. The format is

line
number ___ LET address
name ___ = "message" ___

where a line number goes to the left of the LET, an address name for the alphanumeric scoreboard goes to the right of the LET, and the character string goes to the right of the equals sign. Note that the address name must end with a dollar sign ($) to indicate that a character string is being stored.

For example, a program could contain the following statement:

```
100   LET N$ = "JOE FRIENDLY"
```

Before this statement is executed, there is some message (i.e., some character string) in N$ on the alphanumeric scoreboard. After this statement is executed, the message in N$ is "JOE FRIENDLY" instead of whatever was there before, and the pointer arrow has moved on to the next line of the program.

The statement

```
100   LET N$ = "JOE FRIENDLY"
```

means that the following operations will be performed:

1. Find the message in memory space N$ on the alphanumeric scoreboard.
2. Erase it.
3. Put "JOE FRIENDLY" in the space instead.
4. Go on to the next statement.

TRY IT

What is wrong with the following statement, and how would you correct it?

```
5   LET A = "TRY AGAIN"
```

——————   LET   ————————————————————

The problem is that the computer will try to put a character string into a memory space on the numeric scoreboard—a scoreboard that can only hold numbers. To correct this problem, we can use the alphanumeric scoreboard, as follows:

```
5   LET A$ = "TRY AGAIN"
```

INPUT with Alphanumerics

You may also input information containing alphanumerics using an INPUT statement. The format of the statement is

line number	INPUT	"message"	address name	,	address name	,	address name
————		————	————		————		————

where a line number goes in the blank on the left of INPUT and a list of alphanumeric address names goes after INPUT. There can be one or more address names but they must be separated by commas. When the user types in an alphanumeric string, it must be enclosed in quotation marks in many versions of BASIC.

For example, before the statement

```
10   INPUT "BRAND NAME" B$
```

is executed, the following conditions will exist:

▶ *The computer will have some unknown message in B$ (i.e., a character string in a memory space on the alphanumeric scoreboard).*

After the statement, the computer will be in the following state:

▶ *The computer will have printed out BRAND NAME plus a question mark on the output screen, the user will have typed in a message such as "JUMBOBUTTER" on the keyboard, and this message will be in memory space B$.*

The operations performed by the computer for the statement

```
80    INPUT "BRAND NAME", B$
```

are as follows:

1. Print BRAND NAME? on the output screen.
2. Copy down the user's message on the output screen. (The user will type a message such as "JUMBOBUTTER.")
3. Erase the messages currently in space B$.
4. Put the message (JUMBOBUTTER) in memory space B$.
5. Go on to next statement.

TRY IT

Suppose a program contained the following INPUT statement:

```
20    INPUT "TYPE YOUR NAME" N
```

What is the problem with this statement, and how would you correct it?

_____

_____

_____

_____

The problem is that the subject is likely to enter a character string, but the computer will try to store that in a space in the numeric scoreboard. To correct this problem and to make sure the computer will be able to store anything that the user might enter, we can change the statement to the following:

```
20    INPUT "TYPE YOUR NAME" N$
```

Now the message that the user types will be stored in space N$ in the alphanumeric scoreboard.

PRINT with Alphanumerics

You may also ask the computer to print out the contents of one of its memory spaces holding an alphanumeric message. The format of the statement is

line number	PRINT	"message"	address name	,	address name

where a line number goes in the blank on the left and alphanumeric address names go on the right of PRINT. One or more addresses may be listed, but they must be separated by commas.

Before the statement

```
35   PRINT B$
```

is executed, the condition in the computer is as follows:

▶ *There is a message in memory space B$ (such as JUMBOBUTTER).*

The conditions in the computer after this statement are as follows:

▶ *The same message is still in space B$ and the message is also printed out on a line of the output screen.*

The statement

```
35   PRINT B$
```

means that the following operations will be performed:

1. Find the message from space B$ but do not alter that memory space.
2. Go to the next line of the output screen.
3. Print the message on that line.
4. Go on to the next statement.

TRY IT

Suppose you came across the following statement in a program:

```
20   PRINT "YOUR ANSWER IS X$"
```

What is wrong with this and how would you correct it?

_____

_____

_____

_____

_____

_____

As written, the output of line 20 would be

```
YOUR ANSWER IS X$
```

Since it is likely that the programmer really wanted the computer to print out the string stored in X$, the line should read:

```
20  PRINT "YOUR ANSWER IS" X$
```

Other Statements

Alphanumeric address names may be used with other statements also. For example, one way to use the IF statement is

line number	IF	alphanumeric address name	relation	"message"	THEN	line number

where a line number goes in the first space, an alphanumeric address name goes in the next space, a relational sign (such as *equal to*) goes in the next space, a character string goes in the message space, and a line number goes in the last space. In most versions of BASIC the character string must be enclosed in quotation marks.

For example, the statement

```
12  IF B$ = "JUMBOBUTTER" THEN 999
```

means that before this statement there is some data in memory space B$ and the pointer arrow has just moved to line 12. After this statement, the computer is on line 999 if the data in memory space B$ was JUMBOBUTTER but is working on the next line under 12 if not.

In terms of the operations performed, the statement

```
12  IF B$ = "JUMBOBUTTER" THEN 999
```

means that the following operations will be performed:

1. Check to see what data is in memory space B$ but do not erase it.
2. Compare the data in the space B$ with the data in quotation marks and decide whether they match.
3. If they are the same—letter for letter—then move the pointer arrow to line 999.
4. If they are not the same, move the pointer arrow to the next line next after 12.

TRY IT

Suppose space A$ contains WASHINGTON. What will happen for the following statement?

```
10   IF A$ = "WASHINGTON" THEN 50
```

List the operations that will be carried out.

_____

_____

_____

_____

_____

_____

The operations are as follows:

1. Find the character string in space A$ but do not alter it.
2. Determine whether it matches letter for letter the target string, "WASHINGTON."
3. Since they match, move the pointer arrow to line 50, and continue working down from there.

PROGRAM QUIZ

(1) The ability to store, retrieve, and make decisions based on character strings adds some new flexibility to your program-writing repertoire. For example, write a program to test whether a person knows the capital of some state like California. (Hint: The subject can be asked the question in the form of an INPUT statement.)

_____

_____

_____

_____

_____

_____

Your program should look something like this:

```
20   INPUT "WHAT IS THE CAPITAL OF CALIFORNIA" A$
30   IF A$ = "SACRAMENTO" THEN 50
40   PRINT "WRONG"
45   GO TO 20
50   PRINT "RIGHT"
60   END
```

(2) What goal does the following program accomplish?

```
10   INPUT "YOUR NAME" N$
20   PRINT "HELLO" N$
30   END
```

_____

_____

_____

Briefly describe the operations that will occur in this program.

_____

_____

_____

_____

This program will accept a user's name from the keyboard and then print a greeting to the user on the screen. The operations involved are the following:

1. Print "YOUR NAME" on the screen.
2. Shift control to the keyboard by turning on the WAIT light.
3. The user types in his or her name (e.g., "SUE") and presses the return key.
4. Control shifts back to the program and the RUN light comes on.
5. Print this greeting on the screen: "HELLO SUE."
6. Stop this program and start looking for another.

(3) Write a program that will give a greeting in English, Spanish, or French depending on which language the user asks for. (For

English use, "Good day." For Spanish, use "Buenos Dias." For
French, use "Bonjour.")

_____

_____

_____

_____

_____

_____

Your program could look like this:

```
10   INPUT "TYPE ENGLISH, SPANISH, OR FRENCH" N$
20   IF N$ = "ENGLISH" THEN 60
30   IF N$ = "SPANISH" THEN 70
40   IF N$ = "FRENCH" THEN 80
50   GO TO 90
60   PRINT "GOOD DAY"
65   GO TO 90
70   PRINT "BUENOS DIAS"
75   GO TO 90
80   PRINT "BONJOUR"
90   END
```

(4) Suppose you have the following program:

```
10   INPUT "TYPE ENGLISH, SPANISH, OR FRENCH", N$
20   IF N$ = "ENGLISH" THEN 60
30   IF N$ = "SPANISH" THEN 70
40   IF N$ = "FRENCH" THEN 80
50   GO TO 90
60   PRINT "GOOD DAY"
65   GO TO 90
70   PRINT "BUENOS DIAS"
75   GO TO 90
80   PRINT "BONJOUR"
90   END
```

What would be the output on the screen if the subject typed "GER-
MAN" as the request? _____

What would be the output on the screen if the subject typed "SPANESH" as the request? _____

What would be the output if the subject typed "FRENCH"? _____

For each case tell which lines on the program the pointer arrow will point to.

_____

_____

_____

_____

_____

_____

_____

For "GERMAN" the computer would not print anything on the screen; the pointer would move from 10 to 20 (fails) to 30 (fails again) to 40 (fails again) to 50, then to 90 and stop. For "SPANISH" the same thing would occur. The input fails to match any of the three targets. So you would pay dearly for your spelling error. For "FRENCH," the output will be "BONJOUR." The sequence of the pointer arrow will be 10 to 20 to 30 to 40 (a match is made), to 80, to 90.

Summary

By adding the new alphanumeric memory scoreboard to our computer system, we have increased the kinds of data we can work with. We can now store words or names in memory, we can print out the contents of memory spaces that contain names, we can make decisions based on whether a memory space contains a certain name or not. Thus, while our pocket calculator is limited to numbers, we have now expanded our computer system to include memory for words, names, or other character strings.

Can we use this newfound feature to improve our programs? We have already seen in the Overview to this chapter that the unit price problem could be improved because we can now print out the unit price and the name of the product. We have a similar need in our gradebook problem. As it now stands (see the Summary to the previous chapter), the gradebook program accepts, stores, and prints numbers, but it does not store the student's name that goes with the scores. With our alphanumeric scoreboard we can rectify this problem. The program from the previous chapter is as follows:

```
10   INPUT "SCORE ON EXAM 1" E1
15   INPUT "SCORE ON EXAM 2" E2
20   INPUT "SCORE ON EXAM 3" E3
30   LET A = (E1 + E2 + E3)/3
60   PRINT "EXAM 1 SCORE IS" E1
70   PRINT "EXAM 2 SCORE IS" E2
80   PRINT "EXAM 3 SCORE IS" E3
90   PRINT "AVERAGE SCORE IS" A
100  IF A >= 70 THEN 120
110  PRINT "NOT PASSING"
115  GO TO 10
120  IF A >= 80 GO TO 140
130  PRINT "GRADE IS C"
135  GO TO 10
140  IF A >= 90 THEN 160
150  PRINT "GRADE IS B"
155  GO TO 10
160  PRINT "GRADE IS A"
165  GO TO 10
999  END
```

To include the name of the student along with the grade, we need to add two lines:

```
5    INPUT "STUDENTS NAME" S$
40   PRINT "FOR" S$
```

Thus when we work on the grade for Sam the screen would look like this:

```
STUDENTS NAME? SAM
SCORE ON EXAM 1? 95
SCORE ON EXAM 2? 85
SCORE ON EXAM 3? 75
FOR SAM
EXAM 1 SCORE IS 95
EXAM 2 SCORE IS 85
EXAM 3 SCORE IS 75
AVERAGE SCORE IS 85
GRADE IS B
```

After this the computer would ask for the next student's name.

9

Functions

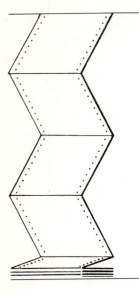

Overview

By now you may think that we have run out of modifications that could be made to improve our computer system. However, we have overlooked a feature that is already a part of many more "expensive" pocket calculators—built-in special functions. For example, in addition to the four arithmetic functions, many calculators will take square roots, generate values for numbers raised to exponents, perform log transformations, or apply geometric formulas. In this chapter we will explore the use of several BASIC functions that you can use in LET statements.

Why are functions needed? Most are useful in very specific situations because they cut down on the number of computations you have to make. For example, if you wanted to raise 2 to the 4th power you could multiply 2 times 2 times 2 times 2 times 2. However, a shorter way to accomplish this goal is to use a single exponent function of the form 2 ↑ 4.

In our unit price problem, we could use special functions to round off our numbers to two places. For example, the program could be revised by adding line 33:

```
10   INPUT "BRAND NAME" B$
15   INPUT "TOTAL COST" T
20   INPUT "NUMBER OF OUNCES" N
30   LET U = T/N
33   LET U = .01 * INT (U * 100 + .5)
35   PRINT B$
40   PRINT "TOTAL COST IS" T
60   PRINT "NUMBER OF OUNCES IS" N
80   PRINT "UNIT COST IS" U
90   IF U ≥ 10 THEN 97
95   PRINT "THATS CHEAP"
97   GO TO 10
99   END
```

In line 33 the unit price is rounded off to the nearest 1/100 of a cent. This rounded-off number is then printed in line 80.

Functions

In Chapter 3 you learned about some of the main arithmetic operations that the computer can perform using its scratch pad:

> addition
> subtraction
> multiplication
> division
> raising a number to a power

In this chapter you will learn several other functions that the computer can perform on your command.

You should think of a function as a formula for taking some number (or numbers) as input and converting it (them) into some number (or numbers) as output. All functions are similar in that a number (or numbers) must be input and a number (or numbers) is output as the result; however, they differ in terms of which formula they use to make the conversion. For example, the SQUARE ROOT function takes a number (like 144) as input and gives its square root as output (12). BASIC generally makes available several functions. Three of the most commonly used are these:

> SQR   Finding the square root of a number.
> INT(X)   Rounding off a number to the highest integer that does not exceed it.
> RND(X)   Generating a random number between 0 and 1.

Let's take a look at how each of these functions can be used.

Square Root Function

The first major function that you will learn about is the **SQUARE ROOT function:**

$$\text{SQR} \left(\begin{array}{c} \text{number or} \\ \text{address name} \end{array} \right)$$

A number or an address name goes in the parentheses. The number you give or the value in the memory space must be a non-negative number, since it is not possible to find the square root of a negative number.

If the SQR function is used in a LET statement, the format would be as follows:

A line number goes to the left of LET, an address name goes to the right of LET, and a number or address name goes in the parentheses.

For example, the statement

```
100   LET X = SQR (144)
```

means that before this statement, there is some number in space X but after this statement the number in space X is the square root of 144 (that is, 12).

The operations performed for the statement

```
100   LET X = SQR (144)
```

are as follows:

1. Find memory space X.
2. Destroy the number in X.
3. Calculate the square root of 144.
4. Put the result in memory space X.
5. Go on to the next statement.

As another example, consider the statement

```
100   LET X = SQR (Y)
```

In this case, before this statement is executed, there is a number in memory space X and a number in memory space Y. After this statement, the same number is still in memory space Y, but a new number is in space X—the square root of the number in Y.

The operations performed for the statement

```
100   LET X = SQR (Y)
```

are as follows:

1. Find the number in space X and destroy it.
2. Find the number in space Y but do not alter it.
3. Calculate the square root of the number in Y.
4. Put that result in space X.
5. Go on to the next statement.

TRY IT

Write a statement to find the square root of 66 and store the result in memory space S.

———— LET ————————

The answer is

```
20  LET S = SQR (66)
```

TRY IT

Suppose the following line was in the program:

```
20  LET X = SQR (100)
```

What would happen to memory space X as this statement is executed?

_____

_____

_____

_____

_____

The old number in X would be erased and replaced with 10.

Rounding Off to an Integer

The next major function is one that allows you to round numbers to an integer. The format is

$$INT \left(\begin{array}{c} \text{number or} \\ \text{address name} \end{array} \right)$$

where a number or address name goes in the parentheses. You must remember that the **INT function** always rounds down to the highest integer that is not greater than the number in the parentheses. Thus INT (1.99) is 1 not 2, INT (−1.99) is −2, INT (0.1) is 0, and INT (−0.1) is −1.

If the INT function is used in a LET statement, the format would be as follows:

$$\underline{\begin{array}{c}\text{line}\\\text{number}\end{array}} \quad \text{LET} \quad \underline{\begin{array}{c}\text{address}\\\text{name}\end{array}} \quad = \quad \text{INT} \left(\begin{array}{c}\text{number or}\\\text{address name}\end{array} \right)$$

A line number goes to the left of the LET and a number or address name goes in the parentheses.

For example, the statement

80   LET C = INT (-33.4)

means that before this statement there is some unknown number in space C but after this statement is executed there is a −34 in space C. (Note that −34 is the highest integer that is not greater than −33.4).

The operations involved for the statement

80   LET C = INT (-33.4)

are as follows:

1. Find the value in memory space C.
2. Destroy that number.
3. Calculate the highest integer not greater than −33.4.
4. Put the answer (−34) into space C.
5. Go on to the next statement.

As another example, the statement

200   LET C = INT (C)

means that before this statement, there is some number in memory space C. After this statement this number has been replaced with the highest integer that does not exceed the value that was in C.

The statement

200   LET C = INT (C)

means that the following operations are performed:

1. Find the number in memory space C (e.g., 55.8).
2. Determine the highest integer that does not exceed this value (e.g., 55).
3. Destroy the old value in C.
4. Put in the new answer.
5. Go on to the next statement.

As noted above, the INT function is limited by the fact that it always gives that integer that is not greater than the number. For example, the INT for 12.999999 is 12 rather than 13. There is a way, however, to make the INT function round off in the expected or conventional way—that is, to round to the next highest number if it is .5 or greater and to the next lowest integer if it is less than .5. This may be accomplished by using the following format:

$$\text{INT} \left(\frac{\text{number or address name} + .5}{} \right)$$

A number or address name goes in the parentheses followed by the plus sign and .5.

For example,

```
100 LET X = INT (Y + .5)
```

would give the following values of X for the following values of Y:

If Y is 12.999 then X is 13 (round down from 13.499).
If Y is 12.001 then X is 12 (round down from 12.501).
If Y is 12.501 then X is 13 (round down from 13.001).
If Y is 12.499 then X is 12 (round down from 12.999).
If Y is 12.500 then X is 13 (13 is an integer already).

Thus when you use the INT function, be sure to use the "plus .5" technique for accurate rounding.

TRY IT

Write a statement that will take the number that is stored in memory space Q and round it to the nearest 100.

————— LET —————————

This can be accomplished by the following statement:

```
10   LET Q = 100 * INT ((Q/100) + .5)
```

You could do the same thing in two statements as follows:

```
10   LET X = Q/100
15   LET Q = 100 * INT (Q + .5)
```

Note that first we see how many 100's are in the number stored in Q, and then we round off to the nearest integer. Thus, if the number in Q was 189, the new value in Q would be 200. This is so because the computer divides 189 by 100 to get 1.89; then .5 is added to yield 2.39, and then the largest allowable integer is 2, which is multiplied by 100 to give 200.

TRY IT

What is accomplished by the following statement? What will be stored in X after the statement is executed? (Suppose X = 2.34789.)

```
10   LET X = (INT (10 * X + .5))/10
```

This statement will take the number stored in X, multiply it by 10, add .5 to the result, then find the integer for that value, and then divide that integer by 10. This gives a running description, but a more concise answer is that this program rounds off the number in X to one decimal point. For X = 2.34789, the result will be that 2.3 is stored in X.

Generating a Random Number

Sometimes you need to randomize things, and a function that can help in this job is the **RANDOMIZE function.** The format is

RND (number or address name)

where a number or address name goes in the parentheses. The output of this function is a decimal number between 0 and 1. (Some versions of BASIC also allow 0 and 1 to be possible outputs.)

If the RND is used in a LET statement, the format is as follows:

line number   LET   address name   =   RND (number or address name)

A line number goes to the left of the LET, an address name goes to the right of the LET, and a number or address name goes in the parentheses.

For example, before the statement

```
50  LET V = RND (1)
```

is executed, there is some number in space V; after this statement, V contains a random decimal between 0 and 1 (such as .7826098).

The operations involved for the statement

```
50  LET V = RND (1)
```

are as follows:

1. Find the number in space V.
2. Destroy it.
3. Generate a random number between 0 and 1 (e.g., .7826098).
4. Put that number in V.
5. Go on to the next statement.

The same sequence of events would occur for

```
50  LET V = RND (X)
```

or any other value placed in the parentheses. However, in some versions of BASIC the same argument (i.e., the same number) placed in the parentheses will give the same random number, while in other versions each generation of a number is entirely random.

One problem with the random-number generator is that it gives decimal fractions as output. You may need to have single-place digits as your output or two-place digits. In order to accomplish this, you may modify the RND function in the following way:

```
INT (10 * RND (1))
```

Any value could go in the parentheses after the RND.

For example,

```
10  LET X = INT (10 * RND (1))
```

means that the following operations will occur:

1. Find the number in space X and destroy it.
2. Generate a random number as specified by RND (1) (e.g., .99567891).
3. Multiply that random number by 10 (e.g., 9.9567891).
4. Determine the highest integer contained in that number (9).
5. Store that number in memory space X.

If you were interested in random integers with two places, you would need to multiply by 100 instead of 10. In this way you can generate integers.

TRY IT

Suppose you wanted a random integer between 0 and 99. Write a statement to generate one and store it in space X.

——— LET ———————————

The statement

```
10   LET X = INT (100 * RND(1))
```

says to generate a random decimal (like .8876099), to multiply it by 100 (like 88.76099), and then round it off (like 88). This allows you to generate random integers between 0 and 99.

TRY IT

Consider the following statement:

```
20   LET S = (INT (10 * RND(1))/10
```

What does this statement tell the computer to do? Suppose that the generated number is .2897890. What would this statement do to the value in S?

———————————————

———————————————

———————————————

———————————————

This statement generates a random number between 0 and 1 (such as .2897890), multiplies it by 10 (such as 2.89789), finds the integer (2), and then divides it by 10 again (.2). Thus this statement takes a random number between 0 and 1 and rounds it to the lowest tenth.

Other Functions

Most versions of BASIC also make available several other functions, in addition to SQR, INT, and RND. Two functions involving signs of numbers are the following:

ABS <u>(X)</u>   Finding the absolute value of a number.
SGN <u>(X)</u>   Giving a -1 if a number is negative, $+1$ if it is positive, and 0 if it is zero.

Two functions involving exponents are the following:

LOG <u>(X)</u>   Giving the natural log of a number (uses the absolute value if the input number is negative).
EXP <u>(X)</u>   Giving the value of e raised to the input number (i.e. the value of e^x) where $e = 2.7182818$.

Four functions used in geometry are the following:

COS <u>(X)</u>   Giving the cosine of a number.
SIN <u>(X)</u>   Giving the sine of a number.
TAN <u>(X)</u>   Giving the tangent of a number.
ATN <u>(X)</u>   Giving the arc tangent of a number.

We have not emphasized these eight functions in this chapter because they are used in specialized situations. However, if you understand how to use the SQR, INT, and RND functions, you should be able to easily learn how to use the other functions by referring to the Style Box below.

STYLE BOX: The BASIC Functions

The eleven BASIC functions are listed below. An example is given for each, the conversion from input to output is summarized, and the limitations are noted.

Function	Example	Input and Output	Limitations
SQR (X)	LET X = SQR (144)	Takes a number as input (144) and gives its square root as output (12).	Numbers must be non-negative.
INT (X)	LET X = INT (−1.99)	Takes a number as input (−1.99) and gives the highest integer that does not exceed that number as output (−2).	Always rounds down to a lower number. Can be adjusted by using INT (X + .5).
RND (X)	LET X = RND (3)	Takes a number as input (3) and gives a random decimal number between 0 and 1 as output (e.g., .67768954).	The output is a decimal fraction. To convert it to an integer, use INT (10*RND (3)).

Function	Example	Input and Output	Limitations
ABS (X)	LET X = ABS (−55.67)	Takes a number as input (−55.67) and gives the absolute value of the number as output (55.67).	
SGN (X)	LET X = SGN (−55.67)	Takes a number as input (−55.67) and gives a −1 if it is negative, +1 if it is positive, and 0 if it is zero.	
LOG (X)	LET X = LOG (100)	Takes a number as input (100) and gives the natural log such that input $= e$ raised to the power given in the output.	
EXP (X)	LET X = EXP (2)	Takes a number as input and gives as output the value of e raised to the input power. (Output equals 2.7182818 raised to the 2nd power in this case.)	
SIN (X)	LET X = SIN (90)	Takes a number indicating angle size* as input and gives sine of that angle as output.	
COS (X)	LET X = COS (90)	Takes a number indicating angle size* as input and gives cosine of that angle as output.	
TAN (X)	LET X = TAN (90)	Takes a number indicating angle size* as input and gives tangent value as output.	
ATN (X)	LET X = ATN (90)	Takes a number as input and gives the angle** as output.	

* Many BASICs require the input data to be in radians rather than in degrees.
** In radians, usually.

Combining the LET and PRINT Statements

In Chapter 2 you learned about PRINT statements and in Chapter 3 you learned about LET statements. You can use LET statements to make computations (even ones with functions), and you can use PRINT statements to print out the results. However, in most versions of BASIC you can combine the LET and PRINT statement into a single shortcut statement. The format for this PRINT statement is

line
number ____   PRINT   formula ____

where a line number goes on the left and the computational formula goes on the right. Any formula that could be used in a LET statement can be used in this super PRINT statement.

For example, the statements

```
10   LET X = (SQR (100))/10
20   PRINT X
```

can be rewritten into one super PRINT statement. As it is written above, line 10 finds the square root of 100, divides it by 10, and stores the result in space X; then line 20 prints the number in space X. To combine these into a super PRINT, the following format would be used:

```
10   PRINT (SQR (100))/10
```

The operations involved for this statement are as follows:

1. Find the square root of 100 and divide that number by 10.
2. Print the answer on the output screen.
3. Go on to the next statement.

Notice that no memory spaces are used in the super PRINT statement, though they are used when a LET statement is involved. Thus the super PRINT gives the same result as LET and PRINT but with less work.

As another example, consider the following statement:

```
20   PRINT (F - 32) * (5/9)
```

In this case, the following operations are involved:

1. Find the number in space F.
2. Subtract 32 from that number, then divide 5 by 9 and multiply the results.
3. Print the answer on the output screen.
4. Go on to the next statement.

Notice again that no memory spaces are needed for storing the answer in this case.

TRY IT

How could you change the following statements to get the same result with just one statement?

```
10   LET X = INT (X)
20   PRINT X
```

─────── PRINT ───────────────────

_____

The answer is to use a super PRINT statement:

```
20   PRINT INT (X)
```

TRY IT

What operations does the computer perform for this statement:

```
10   PRINT RND (X)
```

1. _____

2. _____

3. _____

The following operations are involved:

1. Find a random number between 0 and 1.
2. Print that number on the screen.
3. Go on to the next statement.

Making a Calculator

Suppose you are sitting in front of a computer terminal with a keyboard and a screen. So far we have been assuming that you will be working in the *program mode*; that is, you will write a program and then ask the computer to run the whole thing, or you will call up an old program and ask the computer to run it. (See the Appendix for how to do this.) This mode of operation always involves having a program in the computer's program space, and the computer simply follows the directions one line at a time. When it is finished it will print "READY" on the screen. This means that the computer is ready for the next program.

However, there is a way to obtain "instant service" from the computer. If you write a statement but leave off the line number, the computer will assume you want that statement executed im-

immediate mode   mediately. This is called the **immediate mode** *of operation*. There is no program in the computer. The computer simply does what you tell it to do in a single statement, and when it is finished it prints READY on the screen.

The format for the immediate mode, using a PRINT statement, is

PRINT   "message" or address name or formula
_____

where there is no line number before PRINT, and after it can come a message (in quotation marks), an address name, or a formula.

The following statements will appear on the output screen:

READY	This indicates that the computer will accept a command from the keyboard.
PRINT _____	This is the statement written by you; you must press the return key afterward.
_____	This is the computer's instant response to your statement.
READY	This indicates that the computer is ready for your next command.

For example, the statement

PRINT "HELLO"

entails the following sequence of events:

1. First, there must be a READY on the screen (indicating the computer will accept your statement).
2. Then, your command will appear when you write it.
3. Then you must press the return key, although nothing will appear on the screen. This returns control to the computer (so the RUN light comes back on).
4. The output is printed (HELLO).
5. The task is finished so the computer prints READY on the screen.

So far we have not used the immediate mode to turn the computer into a calculator. Calculations are done using a LET statement but answers are printed out using a PRINT statement. However, when you use the immediate mode you can combine the PRINT and

LET statements into one statement, the super PRINT. (You can also do this using the program mode, as discussed in the previous section.) Some BASICS allow you to enter the formula by itself, without the PRINT, with the identical result. For example, consider the following statement:

```
PRINT (2 * (5-3))/4
```

In this case the computer performs three operations (subtract, multiply, and divide) and then prints the answer. No memory spaces are used. In terms of the sequence of events, the following would occur:

1. First, there must be a "READY" on the screen. (The WAIT light is on.)
2. Then, your statement will appear when you write it from the keyboard.
3. Then you must press the return key (so the RUN light will come on).
4. The computations are executed in the scratch pad in the way described in Chapter 3 (5 minus 3 makes 2, 2 times 2 makes 4, 4 divided by 4 makes 1).
5. The answer is printed on the screen (1).
6. The task is finished so the WAIT light comes back on and "READY" is printed on the screen.

For the statement

```
PRINT  (SQR (100))/10
```

the following operations would occur:

1. First, the "READY" message must be on the screen (and the WAIT light is on).
2. Then, your command is printed on the screen when you type it in from the keyboard.
3. Then you must press the return key to return control to the computer (so the RUN light will come on).
4. Then the computer makes its computations on the scratch pad (the square root of 100 is 10, 10 divided by 10 is 1).
5. The answer (1) is printed on the screen.
6. The "READY" message appears to indicate that the computer is in the WAIT mode.

So far the examples have used numbers only. However, the super PRINT statement may also be used to find the answer to computations involving memory spaces:

```
PRINT  SQR (X)
```

would result in the following sequence:

1. "READY" is on the screen. (The WAIT light is on.)
2. Your command appears when you type it in.
3. You press the return key, and the RUN light comes on.
4. The number in space X is found (e.g., 49).
5. The computation is completed; the square root of 49 is 7.
6. The answer is printed on the screen.
7. "READY" is printed on the screen.

TRY IT

Now that you know how to turn your computer into a calculator, tell what will be printed on the screen for each of the following. Assume that you type them in after the computer prints "READY" on the screen and that the value of X is 9.

```
PRINT   X                        _____
PRINT   2                        _____
PRINT   X + 2                    _____
PRINT   Y = X + 2                _____
PRINT   X + X                    _____
PRINT   3 * 4                    _____
PRINT   (X*2)/(X-5)              _____
PRINT   SQR (X)                  _____
PRINT   SQR (4)                  _____
10  PRINT SQR (9)                _____
PRINT   SQR (8 + 8)              _____
PRINT   INT (SQR (150))          _____
PRINT   INT (RND (1))            _____
PRINT   3 + INT (RND (1))        _____
```

Following are the answers:

```
PRINT X              is 9
PRINT 2              may be an error (could be corrected by
                     enclosing the 2 in quotation marks)
PRINT X 2            is 11
PRINT Y X 2          is an error (could be corrected by
                     enclosing the Y = X + 2 in quotation
                     marks but this may not be what you
                     intended)
PRINT X X            is 18
PRINT                is 12
PRINT X              is 4.5
PRINT SQR X          is 3
PRINT SQR 4          is 2
10 PRINT SQR 9       will not run without a RUN command
```

```
PRINT SQR 8 8    is an error since only one number may be
                 in the parentheses
PRINT INT SQR    is 12
PRINT INT RND    is 0 (since any number between 0
                 and 1 rounds down to 0)
PRINT 3 INT      is 3
```

PROGRAM QUIZ

(1) This chapter has added some power to the kinds of computations you can do with LET statements (and super PRINT statements). Suppose you wanted to find the square root of the first 100 integers. Write a program to accomplish this goal.

_____

_____

_____

_____

_____

_____

_____

Your program could use looping as follows:

```
10   FOR X = 1 TO 100
20   LET Y = SQR (X)
30   PRINT X, Y
40   NEXT
50   END
```

This program will print out an integer and its square root for the first 100 integers.

(2) Suppose you have the following program:

```
10   FOR X = 1 TO 100
20   LET Y = SQR (X)
30   PRINT X, Y
40   NEXT
50   END
```

Modify this program so that it will round off the square roots to integers.

_____

_____

_____

_____

_____

Your answer should involve the INT function.

```
10   FOR X = 1 TO 100
20   LET Y = SQR (X)
30   LET Y = INT (Y + .5)
40   PRINT X, Y
50   NEXT
60   END
```

In line 20 the value of the square root is stored in Y. Then in line 30 the integer is found. You could combine lines 20, 30, and 40 into one super PRINT statement:

```
20   PRINT X = INT (SQR(X)+.5)
```

(3) Write a program to generate 20 random single-digit integers.

_____

_____

_____

_____

The answer could look like this:

```
10   FOR X = 1 TO 20
20   LET Y = RND (X)
30   LET Y = INT (Y * 10)
40   PRINT X, Y
50   NEXT
60   END
```

In this case lines 20, 30, and 40 could be combined into one super PRINT:

```
20  PRINT X = INT (RND (X) * 10)
```

(4) If you were working in the immediate mode, what would be the output for the following statement?

```
LET X = SQR (169)
```

Suppose you now enter a second statement after this one has been executed:

```
PRINT X
```

What would be the output for the second statement?

_____

_____

_____

_____

_____

For the first statement there would be no output. The screen would just say "READY" with no new data output. However, the statement would be executed and 13 would be stored in space X. For the second statement, the output would be 13. The computer would print out the number in memory space X. Thus nothing is printed out in immediate mode unless you use a PRINT; in this example you could have used a super PRINT:

```
PRINT  SQR (169)
```

The result would be a 13 on the screen.

Summary

In this chapter you have learned how to make even more improvements in our computer system—by adding more functions (in addition to the simple arithmetic operations), by combining the LET and PRINT statements into a single statement, and by using the immediate mode. We can use each one of these features with our gradebook problem.

The program as it stands from the previous chapter is as follows:

```
  5   INPUT "STUDENTS NAME" S$
 10   INPUT  "SCORE ON EXAM 1" E1
 15   INPUT "SCORE ON EXAM 2" E2
 20   INPUT "SCORE ON EXAM 3" E3
 30   LET A = (E1 + E2 + E3)/3
 40   PRINT "FOR" S$
 60   PRINT "EXAM 1 SCORE IS" E1
 70   PRINT "EXAM 2 SCORE IS" E2
 80   PRINT "EXAM 3 SCORE IS" E3
 90   PRINT "AVERAGE SCORE IS" A
100   IF A>=70 THEN 120
110   PRINT "NOT PASSING"
115   GO TO 10
120   IF A>=80 GO TO 140
130   PRINT "GRADE IS C"
135   GO TO 10
140   IF A>=90 THEN 160
150   PRINT "GRADE IS B"
155   GO TO 10
160   PRINT "GRADE IS A"
165   GO TO 10
999   END
```

If we want the average test score rounded off to one decimal place, we could add a new line 35. This line could convert the average calculated in line 30 to a number with just one decimal place. How would you do this?

If you used the INT function, your statement could be the following:

```
 35   LET A = .1 * INT(A*10 + .5)
```

In this case if the average value was 85 (based on 95, 85, and 75), the computer would perform the following steps at line 35: 85 times 10 is 850, 850 plus .5 is 850.5, the integer of 850.5 is 850, .1 times 850 is 85.0. Thus the number now stored in space A will be 85.0, and that is what will be printed out at line 90. If the average was 88.333333 (based on scores of 80, 90, and 95) the steps at line 35 would be: 88.333333 times 10 is 883.33333, 883.33333 plus .5 is 883.833333, the integer of this value is 883, and .1 times 883 is 88.3. Thus the value stored in space A will be 88.3.

We could also take advantage of the method for combining the LET and PRINT statements. We could erase lines 30 and 90 and replace them with just one line. What would it be?

One suggestion is:

```
90   PRINT "AVERAGE SCORE IS" (E1 + E2 + E3)/3
```

Do you see any problems with this procedure? One problem is that we have not allowed for rounding off numbers. Another problem is that the average is never stored in memory. While this may not be important in this case, there may be cases when you want to keep a record in memory of each answer you generate.

Finally, you could use your computer as a calculator for generating averages. For Sam you could write the following statement:

```
PRINT (95+85+75)/3
```

The answer would immediately appear on the screen:

```
85
```

Then you could give another immediate mode statement. However, as you can see, the immediate mode can become quite tedious when you have a long list of instructions (such as would be used to assign grades or for a classroom full of students).

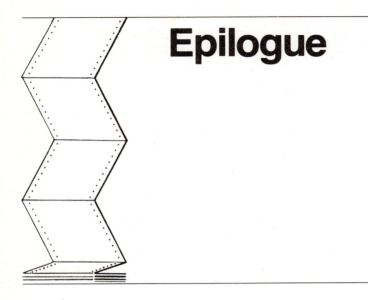

Epilogue

Congratulations! If you have managed to get to this point in the book, you now know the fundamentals of BASIC programming. Take a minute to consider how far you have come.

You began with a little experience you have had with pocket calculators, and you systematically built on that base. First, you learned how to get numbers into and out of the computer's memory (with READ, DATA, and PRINT statements). Then you learned how to instruct the computer to make numerical computations (with the LET statement). Next, you learned how to control the order in which statements in a program are executed (using IF, GO TO, and FOR-NEXT statements). These statements added the power to write programs transferring control. Then you learned how to make your programs interactive (by using INPUT statements). Then you learned how to bring character strings into your programs by using the alphanumeric memory scoreboard. Finally, you polished off your training with the addition of more functions, and you learned how to use the immediate mode to make quick computations. Your progress is summarized in Figure 12, which shows how you progressed on the unit price problem—from calculator to full BASIC program.

*Figure 12   Solutions to the Unit Price
Problem Presented in This Book*

Unit Price Problem

Given total cost and number of units, determine
the unit price of grocery items. For example,
what is the price per ounce of a 12-ounce jar of
peanut butter that costs $1.03?

```
        .08581333
   12 ) 1.03
        96
        70
        60
       100
        96
         4
```

Calculator Operations for Unit Price Problem

1. Enter 103 on the digit keys.
2. Press the DIVIDE key.
3. Enter 12 on the digit keys.
4. Press the EQUALS key.

103

12

8.5833333

Computer Operations for Unit Price Problem

1. Put this number in memory space 1.
2. 103
3. Put this number in memory space 2.
4. 12
5. Divide the number in space 1 by the number
   in space 2, and put the result in space 3.
6. Display the number in memory space 3.
7. That is all.

1	103

2	12

3	8.5833333

8.5833333

BASIC Program to Read-In and Print-Out Data

```
10   READ T, N
20   DATA 103, 12
40   PRINT "TOTAL COST IS" T
60   PRINT "NUMBER OF OUNCES IS" N
99   END
```

```
TOTAL COST IS 103
NUMBER OF OUNCES IS 12
READY
```

BASIC Program for Unit Price Problem

```
10   READ T, N
20   DATA 103, 12
30   LET U = T/N
40   PRINT "TOTAL COST IS" T
60   PRINT "NUMBER OF OUNCES IS" N
80   PRINT "UNIT COST IS" U
99   END
```

```
TOTAL COST IS 103
NUMBER OF OUNCES IS 12
UNIT COST IS 8.5833333
READY
```

Figure 12 (cont.)

BASIC Program for Unit Price Problem with Decision Option

```
10    READ T, N                             TOTAL COST IS 103
20    DATA 103, 12                          NUMBER OF OUNCES IS 12
30    LET U = T/N                           UNIT COST IS 8.5833333
40    PRINT "TOTAL COST IS" T               THATS CHEAP
60    PRINT "NUMBER OF OUNCES IS" N         READY
80    PRINT "UNIT COST IS" N
90    IF U > = 10 THEN 99
95    PRINT "THATS CHEAP"
99    END
```

Looping BASIC Program for Unit Price Problem with Decision Option

```
10    READ T, N                             TOTAL COST IS 103
20    DATA 103, 12, 66, 7                   NUMBER OF OUNCES IS 12
30    LET U = T/N                           UNIT COST IS 8.5833333
40    PRINT "TOTAL COST IS" T               THATS CHEAP
60    PRINT "NUMBER OF OUNCES IS" N         TOTAL COST IS 66
80    PRINT "UNIT COST IS" U                NUMBER OF OUNCES IS 7
90    IF U > = 10 THEN 10                   UNIT COST IS 9.4285714
95    PRINT "THATS CHEAP"                   THATS CHEAP
97    GO TO 10                              OUT OF DATA
99    END                                  READY
```

Advanced Looping BASIC Program for Unit Price Problem with Decision Option

```
 5    FOR C = 1 TO 25                                  TOTAL COST IS 103
10    READ T, N                                        NUMBER OF OUNCES IS 12
20    DATA 103, 12, 66, 7, 79, 9.5 (and so on)         UNIT COST IS 8.5833333
30    LET U = T/N                                      THATS CHEAP
40    PRINT "TOTAL COST IS" T                          TOTAL COST IS 66
60    PRINT "NUMBER OF OUNCES IS" N                    NUMBER OF OUNCES IS 7
80    PRINT "UNIT COST IS" U                           UNIT COST IS 9.4285714
90    IF U > = 10 THEN 97                              THATS CHEAP
95    PRINT "THATS CHEAP"                              :(and so on 23 more times)
97    NEXT C                                           READY
99    END
```

Interactive, Looping BASIC Program for Unit Price Problem with Decision Option

```
10    INPUT "TOTAL COST" T
20    INPUT "NUMBER OF OUNCES" N
30    LET U = T/N
40    PRINT "TOTAL COST IS" T
60    PRINT "NUMBER OF OUNCES IS" N
80    PRINT "UNIT COST IS" U
90    IF U >= 10 THEN 10
95    PRINT "THATS CHEAP"
97    GO TO 10
99    END
```

```
TOTAL COST? 103
NUMBER OF OUNCES? 12
TOTAL COST IS 103
NUMBER OF OUNCES IS 12
UNIT COST IS 8.5833333
THATS CHEAP
:(and so on)
STOP
READY
```

Interactive, Looping BASIC Program for Unit Price Problem with Decision Option and with Alphanumeric Memory

```
10    INPUT "BRAND NAME" B$
15    INPUT "TOTAL COST" T
20    INPUT "NUMBER OF OUNCES" N
30    LET U = T/N
35    PRINT B$
40    PRINT "TOTAL COST IS" T
60    PRINT "NUMBER OF OUNCES IS" N
80    PRINT "UNIT COST IS" U
90    IF U >= 10 THEN 10
95    PRINT "THATS CHEAP"
97    GO TO 10
99    END
```

```
BRAND NAME? JUMBO
TOTAL COST? 103
NUMBER OF OUNCES? 12
JUMBO
TOTAL COST IS 103
NUMBER OF OUNCES IS 12
UNIT COST IS 8.5833333
THATS CHEAP
:(and so on)
STOP
READY
```

Interactive, Looping BASIC Program for Unit Price Problem with Decision Option, Alphanumeric Memory, and Rounding Option

```
10    INPUT "BRAND NAME" B$
15    INPUT "TOTAL COST" T
20    INPUT "NUMBER OF OUNCES" N
30    LET U = T/N
33    LET U = .01 * INT (U * 100 + .5)
35    PRINT B$
40    PRINT "TOTAL COST IS" T
60    PRINT "NUMBER OF OUNCES IS" N
80    PRINT "UNIT COST IS" U
90    IF U >= 10 THEN 10
95    PRINT "THATS CHEAP"
97    GO TO 10
99    END
```

```
BRAND NAME? JUMBO
TOTAL COST? 103
NUMBER OF OUNCES? 12
JUMBO
TOTAL COST IS 103
NUMBER OF OUNCES IS 12
UNIT COST IS 8.58
THATS CHEAP
:(and so on)
STOP
READY
```

You have come to the end of the first round with BASIC. There is much you can do with the BASIC statements you have learned. But there is also much more that can be added. If you want to go on, here are some of the things you will learn in your advanced studies:

how to make up your own functions
how to make up more memory space
how to work with entire files rather than separate memory spaces
how to work with loops inside loops

Each of these could be used to help improve our unit price and gradebook programs. For example, wouldn't it be helpful to store all the grades and names in a "file" in the computer's memory?

New additions are being invented for the BASIC language all the time. The nice thing is that they all build on the fundamental concepts you have used here. The programming language you have learned in this book is "upward compatible"—that is, you can use it as is or you can add to it without changing anything you already know. In BASIC there really may be no limit to how much you can do.

Operating Instructions

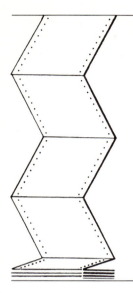

Operating

In this book you learn how to write and interpret BASIC programs. However, you may be wondering how to get your programs into and out of the computer. In other words, you need to be able to tell the computer to put your program into the space for the program list with the pointer arrow pointing to the first statement. This process is accomplished by using "operating instructions."

In this Appendix you will learn about operating instructions for putting a program into the program list space, taking one out, stopping one that is running, saving one for later use, and finding an old program for current use. The commands used for operating instructions are different from the statements learned in the chapters of this book; one of the most obvious differences is that operating instructions do not have line numbers. This tells the computer that they are instructions that should be executed immediately. In fact, the operating instructions are BASIC system commands, and not BASIC statements.

In this Appendix we will assume that you are sitting in front of a terminal with a screen and keyboard. However, the same commands would apply to other modes of interaction, as described in Chapter 1.

File Cabinet

To understand how to get your programs into the computer, it is useful to think of your computer system as containing a file cabinet. Thus, in addition to the five parts of the computer described in Chapter 1, you can add a file cabinet. This file cabinet has all the programs in it. Each program has a simple one-word name, and all the programs are filed in the cabinet in alphabetical order by name. When you write a new program that you want to save in the cabinet you must give it a name, and when you want to find an old program that is in the cabinet you must ask for it by name.

Also, to understand how the operating instructions work, you must think about the part of the computer (described in Chapter 1) that has a space for a program list and a pointer arrow. Each operating command relates to moving a program from the program list space to the cabinet or from the cabinet to the space, or to changing what is in the cabinet.

LOG IN, LOG OUT, and READY

The first thing you must do when you sit down in front of a terminal is to log in. Your center will have its own procedure, and you will just have to memorize it. Essentially, the log-in (or log-on) procedure allows the center to keep track of how much to charge you.

Once you are logged in the screen will show the following:

READY

This means that the computer is waiting for you to give it a command. (The response of some BASICs, such as the Hewlett-Packard BASIC, is "DONE" rather than "READY.") It is your turn.

There are two simple rules that will help you as you sit at a terminal. Rule one is to always keep track of who is in control—when the computer says "READY," it is waiting for you to take control. Rule two is to make sure you have returned control to the computer by pressing the return key after *every* command.

When you are finished working with the computer, there is a LOG-OUT (or LOG-OFF) procedure for stopping the job you are running on your account.

After you have turned on your terminal, logged in, and the screen has displayed "READY," there are two things you can do: you can write a new program and tell the computer to put that into the program list space, or you can tell the computer to use one of the programs from its file cabinet.

OLD Command

The OLD command tells the computer that you want to use a program that it has in its program file cabinet. The format of the command is

```
OLD _____
```

where a name for the program goes in the blank. Note that the command has no line number. This shows that it is not part of any program. After typing in OLD and the name of the old program you want to use, you must return control back to the computer, so press the return key.

For example, for the command

```
OLD COUNT
```

the computer will perform the following actions:

1. Wait for you to press the return key.
2. Go to the program file cabinet and find the program named COUNT.
3. Refile whatever program is currently in the program list space.
4. Copy the COUNT program from the file cabinet into the program list space.
5. Do not destroy the original COUNT program—it will be refiled in the file cabinet after it is used.
6. Return control of the situation to you, by writing READY on the screen.

Note that the computer does not execute the COUNT program. It simply places it into the program list space so that it is ready to run. Note that before this command, there is some unknown program in the program space but after this command that program has been refiled into the cabinet and the COUNT program is in the program list space. In order to have the computer execute your program you must use the RUN command.

NEW Command

The NEW command tells the computer that you are going to write a new program. The format is

```
NEW _____
```

where a name for the program goes in the blank. It is useful to use a name that you can easily identify. Also note that no line number is given. When there is no line number the computer knows that this is an operating instruction. After typing NEW and the name of your program, you must press the return key.

For example, for the command

```
NEW METRIC
```

the computer will perform the following operations:

1. The computer will wait for you to press the return key.
2. Then the computer will refile any program that is now in the program list space.
3. It will put your program in that space with the lines in numerical order.
4. Then the computer will print "READY" on the screen and wait for more keyboard instructions.

Note that the computer does not execute your program. It simply places it in the program list space so that it is ready to run. In order to run it, you must use the RUN command. In order to save it in the file cabinet for future reference, you must use the SAVE command.

LIST Command

Once you have gotten your program into the program list space—either by a NEW or an OLD command—there are several things you can do. If you want to know what the computer has in the program list space, you can use the LIST command. The format is

```
LIST
```

where no line number goes before the command. You must then press the return key to tell the computer whose turn it is.

The computer will then execute the LIST command as follows:

1. The computer will wait for you to press the key.
2. Then it will print out the entire program that it has in its program list space. (This allows you to make sure that you are using the correct program.)
3. Then the computer will return control to the keyboard and print READY on the screen.

Note that the program is still in the program list space after your LIST command.

RUN Command

Once you have gotten the desired program into the program list space, you may want the computer to execute the program. This is accomplished by using the RUN command:

```
RUN
```

There is no line number and no program name. This must be followed by pressing the return key to tell the computer that control is returned to it.

For the command RUN, the computer will perform the following operations:

1. The computer will wait for you to press the return key.
2. The computer will take the program that is currently in the program list space, set the pointer arrow at the first line, and execute the program.
3. Then when the pointer arrow reaches the line that says END, it will print READY and wait for more instructions.

Note that your program is still in the program list space, so if you typed RUN again, it would start over.

STOP and CONT Commands

While the program is running, you may want to interrupt it. For example, there may be an error or a continuous loop. The statement you can use to stop a running program is

STOP

followed by pressing the return key. Most systems will also stop if you press down the control key and the letter C at the same time.

The computer will shift control to you and let you know this by printing "READY" on the screen.

Now you can start over with a new program or old program or list the program. Or you can resume the program you just interrupted by typing in

CONT

which is a shorter way of saying CONTINUE. Then hit the return key and the computer will resume operating at the point where it was interrupted. When finished it will print READY.

SAVE Command

The last command you will learn about for controlling programs is the SAVE command. Once you have written a new program, you may want to LIST it, and RUN it to make sure it is debugged. If you want to keep it in the file cabinet, you need to use the SAVE statement. The format is

SAVE

where no line number or name is used.

For this command the computer will do the following:

1. Make a copy of the program that is currently in the program list space, including its name.
2. Place that program in the program file cabinet under its name.
3. Do not destroy the program currently in the program list space. (You can have it RUN.)
4. Print "READY" to tell the user that another command may be entered.

UNSAVE Command

When the file cabinet gets too crowded, it is time to clean out un-needed programs. There is only a limited amount of space for saving programs. To throw out old programs, the UNSAVE command is used. The format is

UNSAVE _____

where the name of a program goes in the blank and the return key must be pressed. The computer will do the following:

1. Go to the file cabinet and find the program by that name.
2. Destroy that program, thus leaving more space in the file cabinet.
3. Print READY on the screen to tell the user that another command should be entered.

STYLE BOX: All READYs Are Alike

Whenever you see that the computer has printed "READY" on the screen that means that it is waiting for one of the operating instructions. The rule to remember is that all READYs are alike. This means that it does not matter what has gone before; if the computer says READY, it is asking that you just start over by telling it what program to put into the program list space and then what to do with it.

Operating Sequences

There are two common operating sequences that you will use: running an old program and running a new program.

To run an old program you must get the program from the file cabinet to the program list space (by using an OLD command) and then have the computer start work on the program (by using a RUN command). The output screen will show the following sequence:

READY	The computer is waiting for input.
OLD COUNT	You ask for a program called COUNT and press the return key.
READY	The computer finds your program in the file cabinet and puts it into the program space.
RUN	You ask the computer to execute the program.
output . . .	The program is executed and any output is printed on the screen.
READY	The computer is finished and is ready for your next command.

To run a new program you must write the new program (giving it a name), and then execute the program (with a RUN command). The output screen will show the following sequence:

READY	The computer is waiting for input.
NEW COUNT2	You tell the computer to refile any old program that was in the program space and to start putting in a new one, line by line. You press the return key.
READY	The computer now has an empty program list space and is waiting for input.
first line	You give the first line of the program, with a line number, and press the return key.
READY	The computer puts the line in the program list space.
next line	You give the next line of the program and press the return key.
READY	The computer adds this line to the program in the program list space. This process can be repeated until the program is complete.
RUN	You ask the computer to execute the program.
output	The program is executed and any output is printed on the screen.
READY	The computer is finished and is waiting for your next command.
SAVE	You ask the computer to store the program in the file cabinet under the name "COUNT2."
READY	This is done, and the computer is waiting.

In some BASICs, the computer will prompt each next line of your program without the READY message but by simply going on to the next line and awaiting your line number.

Examples and Formats of the BASIC Statements

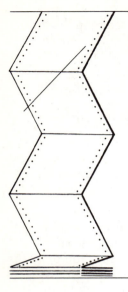

Examples of the Ten BASIC Statements

Statement	Example	Computer Operations
READ	10 READ T, N	Find first two numbers at INPUT WINDOW (103 and 12). Move these numbers through INPUT WINDOW to FINISHED pile. (If there are no numbers in line, print OUT OF DATA and stop.) Store first number in memory space T and second number in memory space N, erasing whatever was there previously. Go on to the next statement.
DATA	20 DATA 103, 12, 66, 7, 79, 9.5	Place the numbers (103 and 12 and 66 and 7 and 79 and 9.5) in line waiting at the INPUT WINDOW. Go on to the next statement.
LET	30 LET U = T/N	Find the number in memory space U and erase it. Find the numbers in T (103) and N (12) but do not erase them. Divide the first by the second and put the result in memory space U. Go on to the next statement.
PRINT	80 PRINT "UNIT COST IS" U	Check to see what number is stored in space U but do not alter it. Print out the message UNIT COST IS followed by the number from space U. Go on to the next statement.

IF	90 IF U >= 10 THEN 10	Find the number in memory space U but do not alter it. Compare it to 10. If it is greater than or equal to 10 move POINTER ARROW to line 10, but if it is not move POINTER ARROW to next statement (line 95).
	95 PRINT "THATS CHEAP"	Move POINTER ARROW from current line (line 97) to line 10, and continue working down from there.
GO TO	97 GO TO 10	
END	99 END	Stop working on this program. Print READY on the screen. Be prepared for new instructions.
FOR	5 FOR C = 1 TO 25	Find memory space C; this will be used as a counter. On first time at line 5, erase the number in space C and put in 1. Compare number in C with exit number (25). If the number in C is 25 or less go on (to line 10) but if it is greater than 25 move POINTER ARROW to line directly below the NEXT statement, ignoring others inbetween.
INPUT	10 INPUT "BRANDNAME" B$	Print out message BRANDNAME followed by question mark. Wait for user to type in message followed by RETURN KEY press. Then store user's message in memory space N$ erasing whatever was there before.
	15 INPUT "TOTAL COST" T 20 INPUT "NUMBER OF OUNCES" N 30 LET U = T/N 80 PRINT N$, U	
NEXT	90 NEXT C	Find number in counter (memory space C) and add step size to it (add 1), destroying the old number in space C. Move POINTER ARROW up to line with FOR on it (line 5).
	99 END	

Formats of the Ten BASIC Statements

Statement	Format	Comment
READ	line number READ address name ___ , address name ___ , address name ___	May have one or more names, separated by commas.
DATA	line number DATA number ___ , number ___ , number ___	May have one or more numbers, separated by commas.
LET	line number LET address name ___ = name or number ___ operation ___ name or number ___	Formula LET. May have one or more operations.
LET	line number LET address name ___ = number ___ operation ___ number ___	Arithmetic LET. May have one or more operations.
LET	line number LET address name ___ = name or number ___	Counter Set LET.
PRINT	line number PRINT "message" ___ address name ___ , address name ___ , address name ___	May have one or more names, separated by commas.
PRINT	line number PRINT address name ___ , address name ___ , address name ___	May have one or more names, separated by commas.
PRINT	line number PRINT "message" ___	
IF	line number IF name or number ___ relation ___ name or number ___ THEN line number ___	
GO TO	line number GO TO line number ___	
END	line number END	
FOR	line number FOR address name ___ = name or number ___ TO name or number ___ STEP number ___	May omit STEP number (both the word STEP and number) if step size is one. Must have a matching NEXT.
INPUT	line number INPUT "message" ___ address name ___ , address name ___ , address name ___	May have one or more names, separated by commas.
INPUT	line number INPUT address name ___ , address name ___ , address name ___	May have one or more names, separated by commas.
NEXT	line number NEXT address name ___	Must be preceded by a matching FOR.

Three Kinds of LET

Counter Set LET	10	LET C = 5
Arithmetic LET	10	LET C = 50/10
Formula LET	10	LET C = T/N / or 10 LET C = T/10

Four Kinds of Transfer of Control

Branching

```
90   IF U  >= 10 THEN 99
95   PRINT "THATS CHEAP"
99   END
```

Repeating a READ

```
10   READ T, N
   .
   .
   .
   .
97   GO TO 10
```

Waiting for a Data Number

```
10   READ T, N
20   DATA 103, 12, 66, 7, .999
30   IF T = .999 THEN 99
   .
   .
   .
   .
97   GO TO 10
99   END
```

Waiting for a Counter.

```
10   FOR C = 1 TO 5
   .
   .
   .
   .
97   NEXT C
```

Two Types of Address Names

Numeric Address Names A, A1, A2, A3, A4, A5, A6, A7, A8, A9, B, B1, B2 . . . and so on

Alphanumeric Address Names A\$, B\$, C\$, D\$ . . . and so on

Three BASIC Functions

Square Root	10	`LET X = SQR (144)`
Integer	10	`LET X = INT (X + .5)`
Random Number	10	`LET X = RND (1)`

Eight Operating Commands

```
OLD      program
         name
         _____

NEW      program
         name
         _____

LIST

RUN

STOP

CONT

SAVE

UNSAVE   program
         name
         _____
```

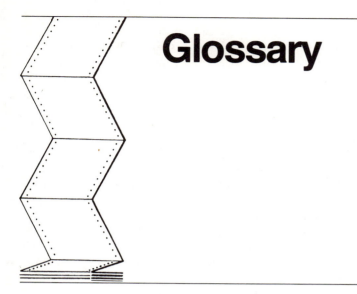

Glossary

Address Name. A symbol used in READ, LET, PRINT, IF, FOR, NEXT and INPUT statements to represent a single location in the computer's memory; consisting of a letter or letter and digit pair, such as A or B9, if the stored information is a number (digit string), and consisting of a letter followed by a dollar sign ($), such as A$ or B$, if the stored information is a sequence of any characters (character string). See also *memory scoreboard, digit string, character string.*

Arithmetic and Logic Component. Part of the central processing unit (CPU), dealing with performing arithmetic and logical operations. See also *input device, output device, memory device, central processing unit.*

Arithmetic LET Statement. A type of LET statement in which a computation is carried out on specified numbers and the result is put into a specified number space. See also *Counter Set LET statement, Formula LET statement.*

BASIC. A programming language developed by Kemeny and Kurtz, which means "Beginner's All-Purpose Symbolic Instruction Code."

Back-up Memory. A device located outside the main computer which stores information, in addition to core memory; also called peripheral memory. See also *memory device, core memory.*

Batch Mode. A mode of presenting instructions and data to a computer in which all information must be presented prior to running the program. See also *interactive mode, immediate mode.*

Body of the Loop. The lines of a looping program that are repeated each time the loop is executed. See also *looping program, reset condition, initial condition, exit condition.*

Branching Program. A program which has two or more alternative routes with both routes starting at a common line and coming together at a common line, and in which no line may be executed more than once. See also *transfer of control, looping program.*

Central Processing Unit (CPU). The central components of the computer which perform arithmetic and logical operations, and which determine the order of execution of instructions. See also *arithmetic and logic component, executive control component, input device, memory device, output device.*

Character String. Information to be stored in memory that may consist of letters, numerals, or digits. Also called alphanumerics. See also *digit string, address name.*

Command. An instruction to the computer that is not part of a program, and which has no line number. See also *statement.*

Computer. A device for the electronic storage, manipulation, and production of symbols, upon command.

CONTROL C. Two buttons (CONTROL Key and C Key) on most terminal keyboards which, if pressed simultaneously, will stop the current program and allow the user to give new instructions. See also *RETURN Key, STOP command.*

Core Memory. A component generally located in the central computer that stores information. Also called main store/memory. See also *memory device, back-up memory.*

Counter Set LET. A type of LET statement in which a specified number is put into a specified memory space. See also *Arithmetic LET statement, Formula LET statement.*

Conditional Branch. A type of transfer of control in which the computer moves from one line of the program to another line under certain conditions, such as indicated in an IF statement. See also *transfer of control, unconditional branch.*

DATA Statement. A BASIC instruction used in conjunction with the READ statements, indicating the information that may be stored into the computer's memory.

Destructive Read-in. The idea that a READ statement always requires that the previous contents of a memory space be erased. See also *non-destructive read-out.*

Digit String. Information to be stored in memory that consists solely of a number. See also *character string, address name.*

END statement. A BASIC instruction that indicates the end of a program.

Error Message. A message that is printed on the output device and which indicates that an error has occurred during the execution of a program.

Executive Control Component. Part of the central processing unit (CPU) concerned with determining the order of execution of statements. See also *arithmetic and logic component, central processing unit, input device, output device, memory device.*

Exit Condition. The condition that must exist in a looping program for the computer to transfer control outside of the loop, such as when a counter reaches a certain number. See also *looping program, reset condition, body of the loop, initial condition.*

Formula LET Statement. A type of LET statement in which a computation is carried out involving address names, and the result is stored in a specified memory space. See also *Counter Set LET, Arithmetic LET statement.*

FOR Statement. A BASIC instruction, used in conjunction with a NEXT statement, for forming loops.

GO TO Statement. A BASIC instruction in which control is transferred to some specified line in the program.

Hardware. The physical components of a computer, such as the keyboard, output screen, memories, electronic circuits, and so forth. See also *software.*

IF Statement. A BASIC instruction in which control is transferred to some specified line in the program only if certain conditions are met.

Immediate Mode. A mode of presenting instructions to a computer in which each instruction is executed immediately after it is entered. See also *interactive mode, batch mode.*

Initial Condition. The state created at the beginning of a loop in a looping program, such as a counter being set to zero. See also *looping program, body of the loop, reset condition, exit condition.*

Input Device. Device for getting information into the computer's memory, such as a terminal keyboard, card reader, magnetic tape reader, magnetic disk reader. See also *output device, memory device, executive control component, arithmetic and logic component.*

INPUT Statement. A BASIC statement which allows users to interact with a running program by entering data from an input device during the execution of a program.

Input Window. An analogy for the input component of the computer, in which a line of numbers is waiting outside a window and each number is moved through the window to a finished pile as it is processed. See also *output screen, memory scoreboard, program list, pointer arrow, scratch pad.*

INTEGER Function. A BASIC operation, which may be used in a

LET statement, and which computes the highest possible integer that does not exceed the specified number. See also *SQUARE ROOT function, RANDOMIZE function.*

Interactive Mode. A mode of presenting instructions and data to a computer in which the user may enter data while the program is running, and which involves INPUT statements. See also *batch mode, immediate mode.*

LET Statement. A BASIC instruction that assigns a specified number or the result of a specified computation to a space in the computer's memory. See also *Counter Set LET statement, Arithmetic LET statement, Formula LET statement.*

Line Number. An integer, usually between 1 and 99999, that must precede each statement in a program, and which indicates the order of statements in a program.

Looping Program. A program which has two or more alternative routes, and in which some of the lines of the program may be executed more than once. See also *transfer of control, branching program.*

Machine Language. The internal language of the computer into which the instructions from a programming language must be translated. See also *programming language.*

Memory Device. A device for the storage of information, including core memory and back-up memory devices. See also *core memory, back-up memory, output device, input device, executive control component, arithmetic and logic component.*

Memory Scoreboard. An analogy for the memory components of the computer in which information may be written on labelled chalkboards. See also *input window, output screen, program list, pointer arrow, scratch pad.*

Message. A sequence of characters, produced on the output device, which may be a part of a PRINT or INPUT statement.

NEXT Statement. A BASIC statement used in conjunction with the FOR statement, for forming loops.

Nondestructive Read-out. The idea that a PRINT statement never causes the contents of a memory space to be erased. See also *destructive read-in.*

Number. In BASIC, a number that is used in DATA, LET, PRINT, IF, FOR or INPUT statements consists of digits, can have a minus (−) sign in front of it, can have a decimal point (.), and can be in scientific notation (E).

Operational Symbols. Symbols allowed in LET statements, which represent arithmetic operations including addition (+), subtraction (−), multiplication (*), division (/), raising to a power (↑), and use of a function. See also *relational symbols, SQUARE ROOT function, INTEGER function, RANDOMIZE function.*

Operating Instructions. A type of command, not part of a program, which is used in preparing, storing, retrieving, and executing programs; including the OLD, NEW, LIST, RUN, STOP, CONT, SAVE, and UNSAVE commands. See also *command*.

Output Device. A device for communication from the computer to the outside world such as a terminal screen, printer, or card punch. See also *input device, memory device, arithmetic and logic component, executive control component*.

Output Screen. An analogy for the output component of the computer in which messages are printed on successive lines of a scrolling screen. See also *input window, memory scoreboard, program list, pointer arrow, scratch pad*.

Pointer Arrow. An analogy for the executive control component of the computer, in which an arrow points to the line that is currently being executed in a program list. Also see *input window, output pad, memory scoreboard, program list, scratch pad*.

PRINT Statement. A BASIC instruction for getting information from the computer's memory to an output device, such as a screen.

Program. A list of instructions, written in a programming language.

Program List. An analogy for the executive control component of the computer, in which instructions are written as a numbered shopping list or recipe. See also *input window, output pad, memory scoreboard, pointer arrow, scratch pad*.

Programming Language. An English-like language designed for people to give instructions to a computer, and which can be translated into machine language, such as BASIC, FORTRAN, APL, PL/1, COBOL, SNOBOL, LISP, ALGOL, PASCAL. See also *machine language*.

RANDOMIZE Function. A BASIC operation which may be used in a LET statement, and which generates a random number. See also *SQUARE ROOT function, INTEGER function*.

READ Statement. A BASIC instruction for getting information from a DATA statement into a computer's memory.

Relational Symbols. Symbols used in IF statements indicating logical relations, such as $>$ for greater than, $>=$ for greater than or equal, $=$ for equal, $<=$ for less than or equal, $<$ for less than. See also *operational symbols*.

Repeating a READ-in Loop. A type of looping program in which the body of the loop is repeatedly executed until the program runs out of data. See also *looping program, Waiting for a Data Number Loop, Waiting for a Counter Loop*.

Reset Condition. The statements in a looping program for starting another cycle through the loop, such as moving control back to the start of the loop. See also *looping program, body of loop, initial condition, exit condition*.

RETURN Key. A button labeled "RETURN" on most keyboards, which is used when entering data in conjunction with an INPUT request. See also CONTROL C.

Scratch Pad. An analogy for the arithmetic and logical components of the computer, in which computations and logical comparisons are carried out. See also *input window, output screen, memory scoreboard, pointer arrow, program list.*

Software. The instructions for operation of the computer, such as a program. See also *hardware.*

Stand-alone Computer. A situation in which a user is the only person using a computer, such as with a personal computer. See also *time sharing.*

Statement. An instruction to the computer that is part of a program, and which is indicated by a line number; such as the READ, DATA, PRINT, END, LET, IF, GO TO, FOR, NEXT, and INPUT statements. See also *command.*

STOP Command. An instruction entered from an input device which interrupts execution of a running program, and which can be used in conjunction with an INPUT request.

SQUARE ROOT Function. A BASIC operation which may be used in a LET statement, and which computes the square root of any specified number.

Terminal Keyboard. A set of buttons or switches, usually resembling an expanded typewriter keyboard, used for manually entering instructions and data into the computer. See also *terminal screen, input device.*

Terminal Screen. A video display, usually resembling a TV screen, used for outputting information from the computer. Also called CRT or cathode ray tube. See also *terminal keyboard, output device.*

Time Sharing. A situation in which a user shares a large computer with other users, as in a computing center. See also *stand-alone computer.*

Transfer of Control. Involves moving from one line of a program to another line of a program, as indicated in IF, GO TO, and FOR-NEXT statements. See also *conditional branch, unconditional branch, branching program, looping program.*

Unconditional Branch. A type of transfer of control in which the computer must under all conditions move from one line of the program to another line of the program that is not necessarily the next line, such as indicated in a GO TO statement. See also *transfer of control, conditional branching.*

Waiting for a Counter Loop. A type of looping program in which the body of the loop is repeatedly executed until a counter reaches some specified value. See also *looping program, Repeating a READ-in Loop, Waiting for a Data Number Loop.*

Waiting for a Data Number Loop. A type of looping program in which the body of the loop is repeatedly executed until a specified data number is read into the computer's memory. See also *looping program, Repeating a READ-in Loop, Waiting for a Counter Loop.*

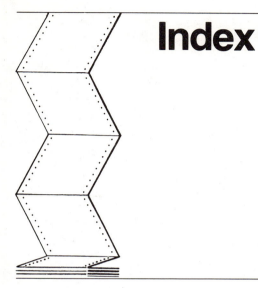

Index